I0817452

BASKET★BALL

Words and Paintings by

KADIR NELSON

L B
100 YEARS
LITTLE, BROWN AND COMPANY
New York Boston

ALSO BY **KADIR NELSON**

We Are the Ship: The Story of Negro League Baseball
words and paintings by Kadir Nelson

Moses: When Harriet Tubman Led Her People to Freedom
by Carole Boston Weatherford, illustrated by Kadir Nelson

Abe's Honest Words: The Life of Abraham Lincoln
by Doreen Rappaport, illustrated by Kadir Nelson

Kobe Bryant of the Los Angeles Lakers

Special thanks to the team at Little, Brown Books for Young Readers: my editor Andrea Spooner, art director Saho Fujii, copy editor and fact-checker Sherri Schmidt, proofreaders Daniel Letchworth and Ariana dos Santos, production editor Jake Regier, additional fact-checker Matt Zeysing, Stephanie Lurie, and Claude Johnson and the Black Fives Foundation.

About This Book

The paintings for this book were done in oil on linen and panel. This book was edited by Andrea Spooner and designed by Patrick Collins, with art direction by Kadir Nelson and Saho Fujii. The production was supervised by Nyamekye Waliyaya, and the production editor was Jake Regier. The text was set in Avenir Book, and the display type is Block Gothic RR Bold Extra Condensed.

 • Little, Brown and Company • Hachette Book Group • 1290 Avenue of the Americas, New York, NY 10104 • Visit us at LBYR.com • First Edition: January 2026 • Little, Brown and Company is a division of Hachette Book Group, Inc. The Little, Brown name and logo are registered trademarks of Hachette Book Group, Inc. • The publisher is not responsible for websites (or their content) that are not owned by the publisher. • Little, Brown and Company books may be purchased in bulk for business, educational, or promotional use. For information, please contact your local bookseller or the Hachette Book Group Special Markets Department at special.markets@hbgusa.com. • Library of Congress Cataloging-in-Publication Data • Names: Nelson, Kadir, author, illustrator. • Title: Basket ball / words and paintings by Kadir Nelson. • Other titles: Basketball Description: First edition. | New York, N.Y. : Little, Brown and Company, 2026. | Includes bibliographical references and index. | Audience: Ages 8–12 | Summary: "An illustrated history of basketball, highlighting the impact that Black players have had on the sport." —Provided by publisher. • Identifiers: LCCN 2023051290 | ISBN 9780316209403 (hardcover) • Subjects: LCSH: Basketball—History—Juvenile literature. | African American basketball players—History—Juvenile literature. | National Basketball Association—History—Juvenile literature. • Classification: LCC GV885.1 .N44 2025 | DDC 796.323—dc23/eng/20232023 • LC record available at https://lccn.loc.gov/2023051290 • ISBNs: 978-0-316-20940-3 (hardcover), 978-0-316-60373-7 (ebook) • PRINTED IN DONGGUAN, CHINA • APS, 9/25 • 10 9 8 7 6 5 4 3 2 1

Title page: Diana Taurasi of the Phoenix Mercury faces off against Tamika Catchings of the Indiana Fever

*This book is dedicated to my wife,
my champion, and my life partner, Dr. Jungmiwha Bullock Nelson.
Thank you for your unyielding love and support. I love you.*

This book is also dedicated to my uncles Michael, Darrell, Brian, Gaffney, and Rodney; my brother Amin; my cousins Brian, Gaffney, Kareem, Blair, David, Aileah, and Kera; my daughters Amel and Aya; my son Ali; my friends Bernard, Ivan, Daron, and Rashard; my former coaches Rodney, King, Marshall, and Les; Biz, Stitch, Bobby, and each of my former teammates; and all I have ever shared a court with who love the great game of BASKET BALL. Ball up.

Charles Barkley of the Philadelphia 76ers laces up

CONTENTS

PREGAME

The Beginning

"I've got it!" —Dr. James Naismith, inventor of basketball

None of us were there in the beginning. That very game, played well over a century ago. It took place on December 21, 1891, in the old gymnasium at the International YMCA Training School, a religious institute in Springfield, Massachusetts. The ball was made of dark brown leather, and the players—nine on each team—stood midway between two wooden baskets that were nailed to the balconies on either side of the court. The game began with a jump ball tossed up by the game's inventor, Dr. James Naismith, a physical education teacher from Canada. At the time, he was an instructor who'd been tasked with creating an indoor sport for his "incorrigible" student athletes to play inside during the cold New England winter. The contest lasted thirty minutes, and it ended with a final score of 1 to 0 (each basket was worth one point). When it was over, Dr. Naismith's students were hooked on the brand-new game, which they later christened *basket ball*.

Basket ball spread fast. A few days after that first game, Dr. Naismith's students went home for winter break and introduced it in *their* hometown YMCAs. Other Ys around the country soon followed suit, putting up baskets and posting Dr. Naismith's rules of the game in their gymnasiums. Within a year, there were Jewish, Italian, and Irish neighborhood teams, and YMCA and other amateur leagues. Then college and professional leagues sprang up all over the Northeast and Midwest. Both men and women took up the new game.

For the first ten years, however, basket ball was confined to white-owned indoor gymnasiums like the YMCA or private athletic clubs—places that were not open to African Americans. But Black folks would get swept up in the game soon enough.

Dr. James Naismith, inventor of basketball

In 1904, an African American fellow by the name of Edwin B. Henderson attended a summer physical education program at Harvard University, where he learned the new game. He returned from the training and taught the game to his students in the segregated school system of Washington, DC. We call Doc Henderson the father of Black basketball because he introduced the game to African Americans in a big way. After that happened, my young friends, the sport would never be the same, because over the next forty years, while professional basket ball remained segregated, we would develop our own style of playing it. And later, when the owners in pro ball were ready to open the door to us, we would help shape it into what it was meant to be—the all-American game. Basketball.

EARLY BASKETBALL

"The sole object of the gentle pastime was to toss the ball in the basket of the other team and stop them from tossing the ball in our basket."

—Marvin A. Riley, newspaperman in Trenton, New Jersey

Nowadays, basketball is lightning fast and chock-full of high scores, high-flying slam dunks, and three-point shots taken from twenty-two to more than forty feet away from the basket. Back in the early 1900s, though, there wasn't any of that. Dr. Naismith's original set of thirteen rules encouraged sportsmanlike play with little to no physical contact: "No shouldering, holding, pushing, tripping, or striking in any way the person of an opponent shall be allowed." Many of the rules still apply, but let me tell you, basketball has changed. The game looked a *whole* lot different back then.

Above: Dr. Edwin B. Henderson, "the father of Black basketball"
Right: Early basketball game at the YMCA in Springfield, Massachusetts

THE SLOW GAME

Early basketball was, as we like to say, similar to classical music: measured, deliberate, and rigid. The game was S-L-O-W, and if a team scored thirty points in a single game, it was really doing something. In the 1890s through the 1920s, basketball looked a lot like a game of keep-away. Pass, pass, pass, and pass some more. Most teams ran soccer-style passing patterns or simple figure-eight, pass-and-weave offenses. Games were called by referees and—get this—*umpires*. Defenders smothered ball handlers, forcing them to get rid of the ball as soon as they got it, so open shots were hard to come by. Final scores were usually in the ten-to-twenty-point range. After every made basket, there was a center jump ball. (The rule changed in 1937 so that, after each basket, the other team gained possession of the ball, which sped up the game.) Shooting the ball was a flat-footed, two-handed event, usually heaved from the chest or thrown underhand. There were no backboards behind the basket, at first, so the ball had to go in clean. There was no dribbling, very little running, no jump shooting, and no fast breaks. And slam-dunking? Hmm…that wasn't even a thought yet.

THE BALL

The very first ball used was a leather *soccer* ball. A special ball was created for the game a few years later, made out of four pieces of smooth brown leather hand-stitched together, then glued over a rubber bladder and closed up with leather laces that protruded from one side. It looked kind of like a big, round football. It was a little larger and heavier than the ball used today, and not really made for dribbling. Since they were handmade, no two basketballs were exactly alike. The ball got pretty heavy and slippery when wet with perspiration, and when it landed on the laces, it took crazy bounces. It was often lopsided by the end of the game. Smaller, lighter, and more uniform unstitched basketballs weren't used until the 1930s.

THE BASKET

The first baskets were literally old farm baskets—the kind used for carrying peaches or apples—that the school's janitor had stored in a closet. They were nailed to opposite sides of the gymnasium balcony track, about ten feet from the floor (ten feet is still regulation height for the basket), and they didn't have holes in the bottom. That meant the game had to come to a complete stop every time a basket was made so someone could climb a ladder and fish out the ball. Over the next few years, the basket changed, first getting a hole in the bottom big enough to allow for poking the ball out with a broomstick, then becoming an iron rim with a closed net, and finally having open laces so the ball could fall straight through. Backboards were added in 1895, not to aid with scoring, mind you, but to prevent spectators sitting behind the basket from interfering with the ball after it was shot, which was a common occurrence. The first backboards were wire mesh; later they were made out of wood or glass.

Soccer ball and peach basket

THE COURT

Some of the first courts used were in private athletic clubs, schools, or church basements, and they often had obstacles and hazards like fireplaces, overhanging balconies, broilers, hot steam pipes, and even steel pillars right in the middle of the floor. Others, in wide-open halls, armories, or auditoriums, were hazard free. Many of the early professional basketball courts were small—typically about sixty-five feet long and thirty-five feet wide, which is less than half the size of today's regulation professional courts. (Official boundaries were set in 1904.) The original positions were forward, center, and back (the guard position was added later), and the number of players per team depended on the size of the court, which could vary considerably. Initially, there was no limit to the number of players on the floor, so the court could get pretty crowded and out of hand. (In 1897, five-player teams, called fives, became the rule.) There were no coaches to control gameplay and help with strategy.

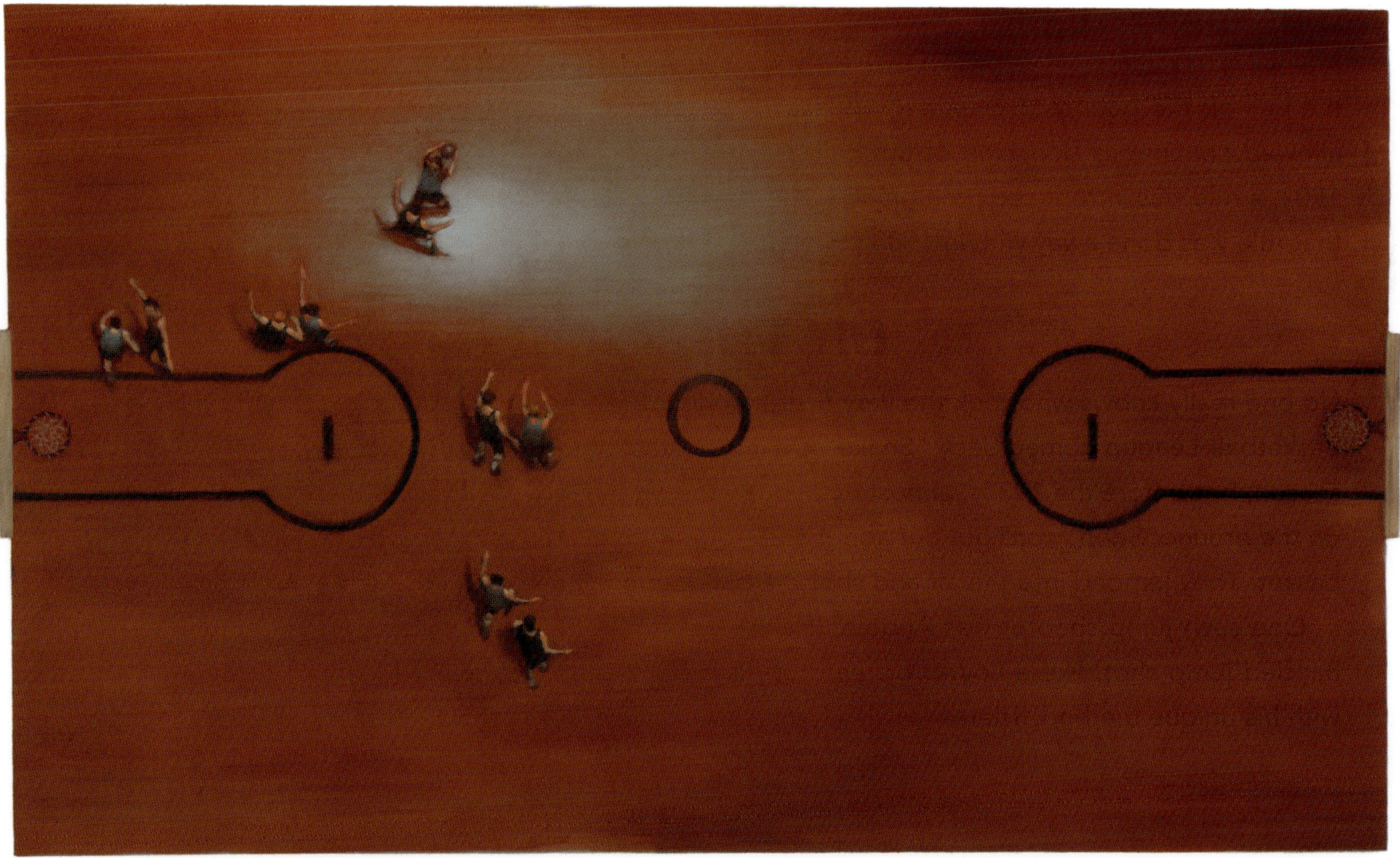

Left: Edwin B. Henderson while playing for the Washington 12 Streeters
Above: Early basketball court

THE UNIFORMS

Early basketball uniforms weren't really uniform. Players wore everything from trousers and tights to tracksuits and football pads. Jerseys were made of light wool, which made them hot and itchy, and they were either long- or short-sleeved and fastened at the bottom with buttons, like baby onesies. They got pretty heavy with sweat by the end of a game, so players dried them out on hotel radiators or in the wind from open bus windows when traveling between games. Players wore shorts held up by leather belts, and often they had to use kneepads because gymnasium floors weren't always level or smooth. Nowadays, players wear fancy sneakers with all kinds of padding and support, but the earliest players wore simple leather-soled shoes with leather tops and, later, rubber-soled shoes with canvas tops.

THE DRIBBLE GAME

Dribbling started kind of by accident. In the original rules, it wasn't allowed. Eventually, players began bouncing or rolling the ball when they were guarded too closely, and they realized they could control the ball off the bounce. By the mid-1890s, college teams began playing a version of the game that allowed continuous bouncing of the ball; the practice caught on and soon became widespread. In 1901, a rule was introduced prohibiting someone who had dribbled the ball from shooting it, too, but that rule was done away with in 1908.

ON THE JUMP

No one really knows who took the very first jump shot. There's a story of a player in the old National Basketball League named Jack "Snake" Deal, who took shots "on the jump" back in the 1901–02 season, but before the 1930s, almost everybody tossed the ball upward with their feet firmly planted on the ground. Soon, word got out about a few guys who had a new method of putting the ball in the basket. They jumped into the air and shot the ball with one hand, all in the same motion.

One such jump shooter was Angelo "Hank" Luisetti, from San Francisco. He had a running one-handed jump shot, like a floater or teardrop, and burned up the college leagues in the mid-1930s with his unique method. There was also Kenny Sailors, who played for the University of Wyoming. He

Cumberland Posey of the Monticello Athletic Association of Pittsburgh, one of the game's first long-range sharpshooters

developed a modern-looking one-handed jump shot around the same time as Luisetti, releasing the ball at the peak of his vertical jump. He used it to help his team win the National Collegiate Athletic Association (NCAA) championship in 1943. Several others shot this way, too, including Glenn Roberts, John "Bud" Palmer, John "Mouse" Gonzalez, John Miller Cooper, and Belus Van Smawley. Jumpin' Joe Fulks popularized the jump shot in the pros. They all had such success with their new way of scoring that, by the 1950s, jump shooting had become standard practice. Next to the dribble, it was the most important innovation in basketball since the game was invented. From then on, basketball happened both on the ground *and* in the air.

TWENTY-FOUR SECONDS

From early on into the 1950s, stalling was a common tactic. A team with the lead would hold the ball without trying to score until the clock ran out. The team in the deficit had to try to foul and force a change of possession. Stalling made basketball games *very* boring for spectators. Nobody wanted to pay to watch a team play a glorified game of hot potato, repeatedly get fouled, and then shoot free throws for the last ten minutes. Officials tried to fix the problem in 1932 by adding a half-court line as well as a ten-second limit for getting the ball across it. Yet still the stalling continued, which led to lower game attendance and less cash flow for pro teams.

At the start of the 1954–55 season, a twenty-four-second shot clock was introduced in the pros. It limited the time a team had to shoot during each possession. If the ball wasn't in the air by the time the shot clock ran out, the offense had to turn the ball over to the other team. That did the trick! The shot clock thwarted fourth-quarter stalling and fouling, dramatically increased scoring and the pace of the game, and brought back paying customers. It saved basketball and brought it into the modern era. The stage was now set for fast breaks and buzzer beaters.

Left: Young Kenny Sailors of the University of Wyoming shoots a jumper
Right: Early shot clock

FIRST QUARTER

The Old School

THE PROS

"Like the rest of the fellows, I'd play where the money was."

—JOE LAPCHICK, BOSTON CELTICS

In 1896, a newly formed basketball team in Trenton, New Jersey, and the Brooklyn YMCA team, both all white, squared off for the first-ever professional basketball game, meaning that it was the first game where players were paid to play. It was a rout. The Trenton team won the game by a score of 16 to 1. Two years later, Trenton joined the world's first organized league of professional basketball teams, the National Basketball League (NBL). Other leagues followed throughout the eastern United States, but most lasted only a few seasons at best before going out of business due to poor organization or lack of money. It didn't help that players routinely jumped from team to team in search of better pay. Sometimes entire teams jumped to different leagues for the same reason. It was hard to maintain attendance when fans couldn't keep track of their favorite players and teams.

Couldn't really blame the players, though. In the early days, professional basketball wasn't exactly a solid career choice. Of the nearly fifty men's professional leagues that operated between 1898 and 1949, only eight survived more than six seasons. It wasn't uncommon for teams to fold only weeks or months into the season, leaving players scrambling to find somewhere else to play. Don't get me wrong—playing basketball was much more enjoyable than doing manual labor, for sure, but team owners were often slow to pay, or sometimes didn't pay at all. During the late 1890s through the 1940s, players were generally compensated on a per-game basis, anywhere from about $1.25 to $150

Basketball game in a cage, circa 1910

a game. One hundred and fifty bucks per game wasn't bad in those days, but it wasn't a sure thing that players would play a full season. Most guys still had to work other jobs in the off-season, which was commonplace until the late 1960s.

Also, for much of the regular season, teams played on the road, which was always an adventure. Most teams traveled by train or on their own bus, if they could afford one, and none of it was easy. The seats on buses and trains were made for people much smaller than the tall basketball players. Guys had to squeeze into those little spaces or stretch their long legs over the tops of seats or across aisles, often for several hours at a time, only to play a game that same evening. And making it to some of those little country towns was a real challenge. For example, a team coming from Rochester, New York, playing in Fort Wayne, Indiana, couldn't take the train all the way. The only stop anywhere near Fort Wayne was about twenty miles from town, somewhere next to a cornfield. The players had to get out and walk to the middle of a little nearby town and pay ten bucks to catch a ride from some high school kid with a car. Air travel wasn't a reliable or particularly safe option until the 1970s. If teams wanted to travel by plane, they had to trust their luck on propeller planes and pray to the good Lord that they would land safely, especially in rough weather.

Professional games in those days were rough, too. They were a lot like modern-day ice hockey games or wrestling matches. Fans were rowdy, and they crowded the court. They spat and threw bottle caps at players and referees, frequently tripped players with their feet or umbrellas, or poked visiting players with hairpins. Some even put out their cigars on players who were wrestling for the ball or taking the ball out after a foul.

Fighting was common. There were scraps at just about every game. Since whoever touched an out-of-bounds ball first got

Traveling players for the New York Renaissance Big Five, also known as the Harlem Rens, 1920s

to throw it in, players duked it out over possession. Sometimes there were even scuffles in the stands. Metal fencing or rope netting had to be put up around the court to separate the crowd from the players because it was just too dangerous otherwise. The barrier also helped speed up the game, since it kept the ball in play and no time was lost chasing the ball into the stands. It's why old-school pro basketball players are often called cagers.

The college game was very different from the pros. There were no cages, and gameplay was much cleaner and faster. Players relied on quickness and wit rather than brute force and dirty tricks. But until the 1930s, when college basketball became more popular, the "rough-and-tumble" professional game was what fans wanted to see. Inside the cage, the key (or lane) was only six feet wide, less than half as wide as the paint nowadays, and it was always crowded. Players trying to score lowered their heads and pounded the ball into the floor with a two-handed dribble and charged their way through defenders to the basket. A discontinued dribble (also called a double dribble) was allowed then, and pushing, head butting, and closed-fist punches were considered savvy moves. When players got the ball, they wouldn't hold it for long, because if they didn't get rid of it quickly, they could get roughed up pretty bad. Players attempting to shoot were usually pushed into the cage, and they often suffered injuries like lost teeth, broken noses, and terrible gashes as a result. It was so rowdy, the lone referee wouldn't even go in there for jump balls. Instead, he stayed on the sideline and tossed the ball over the cage, like a piece of meat thrown to dangerous animals, and let the players fight over it. By the early 1930s, the cages were phased out and a second referee was added.

The first team to dominate the game was the Original Celtics, composed of players from New York City's old Irish neighborhoods. The team began as the New York Celtics but changed its name when a new promoter took over after World War I. The Original Celtics were primarily barnstormers, a traveling team that took on all comers around the Northeast and the Midwest. Drawing as many as eleven thousand spectators for a game, they became the most popular basketball team in the country. They rarely lost, and they set a high standard for solid fundamental basketball. These were basketball scientists, practicing all the time, constantly improving offensive tactics, and devising new methods of scoring, including the "post play," where the center (usually the tallest player on the team) held the ball near the free-throw line and then passed it to a player cutting toward the basket for an open shot. They were the first to use zone defenses, a system in which a defender covers only an allotted section of the court, only guarding opponents who enter their assigned area. They also played

man-to-man defense, a tactic where defenders are assigned to cover and follow only one opponent at a time. Among other strong teams, like the Philadelphia Sphas, the New York Whirlwinds, the Knights of Columbus team in Fort Wayne, and the Trenton Royal Bengals, the Original Celtics were the best all-white professional basketball team during the 1920s, boasting a record in the 1922–23 season of 193 wins, 11 losses, and 1 tie. In 1926, the Original Celtics joined the American Basketball League, but not long after, they were broken up and the players were distributed among other teams.

The pros remained hardy through the 1920s and got a lot tougher in the fall of 1929. On Tuesday, October 29, the US stock market crashed. Lord knows why they had to call it Black Tuesday, but thousands of companies went bankrupt and had to let go of their employees. This led to the Great Depression, a time when as many as one-quarter of American workers lost their jobs. Many ended up on the street. People who were able to find work no longer had money to spend on things like movies or basketball games. Pro basketball was in trouble, and most of the white professional leagues folded. Black basketball, on the other hand, was just getting started.

THE BLACK FIVES

"The ball can travel faster by air than by dribble."

—William "Pop" Gates, New York Renaissance Big Five

Today, there are so many African Americans in the game you'd think we invented it. But the truth is, basketball wasn't an immediate hit with us. In fact, at the turn of the twentieth century, many of our young folks thought the game wasn't rough enough. They preferred football or baseball. After Dr. Henderson introduced basketball to Black DC schools in 1904, it took a few years for the game to take hold across the country, and another few before the first Black professional basketball team stepped onto the court in 1910.

There were other factors at play as well. Starting in 1877, only fourteen years before basketball was invented, Black and white people in the southern United States were forced to live separately for almost ninety years. Libraries, restaurants, schools, movie theaters, stores, public bathrooms, water fountains, and other places were segregated by what were called Jim Crow laws. Basketball was segregated, too, at first. There were white basketball teams, and there were teams made up of only African Americans, called Black fives.

Alpha Physical Culture Club basketball team, 1900s

By the mid-1910s, the face of America was changing. African Americans from the rural South were migrating in big numbers to cities like New York, Philadelphia, Los Angeles, Chicago, and others in the North and West, where there were better opportunities for employment and education. The North didn't have Jim Crow laws, and so—even with the exception of some establishments that were segregated anyway—there were more places where Black folks could learn, play, and watch sports. Cities like Detroit, Chicago, and New York, in particular, were quickly becoming centers for Black culture, and they would eventually be where some of the best basketball in the country was played.

Although Black basketball was born in Washington, DC, it grew up in Harlem, New York City. By as early as 1905, basketball had made its way north and taken hold in the city's West Indian communities. Inspired by the physical-fitness movement of the late 1880s, which promoted strengthening of the mind, body, and spirit as a way to achieve good health, a group of mostly island-born fitness enthusiasts, including Jamaican-born brothers Conrad, Gerald, and Clifton Norman, founded the Alpha Physical Culture Club in 1904, the nation's first all-Black fitness club. The Normans were fine athletes, educated, and well-known among New York City's Caribbean-born elite, and by 1906 they were arranging sports competitions with two other Black athletic organizations: the St. Christopher Club of Manhattan and the Smart Set Athletic Club of Brooklyn.

In 1907, the Smart Set formed the first organized amateur all-Black basketball team. The St. Christopher Club quickly followed suit, and soon the two teams were scrimmaging each other. Later that year, the all-Black Olympian Athletic League was formed and held the first fully organized basketball game between two African American teams: the St. Christopher Club and a brand-new team called the Marathon Athletic Club. The St. Christophers won that first league game by a convincing score of 31 to 1, but it was the Smart Set who went undefeated that season, claiming the first Black amateur basketball championship. The next year the Alpha Physical Culture Club replaced the Marathons, and the league expanded to six teams. By 1910, the world's first all-Black professional basketball team, the New York All Stars, was formed in—you guessed it—Harlem. Primarily a traveling team, the New York All Stars played for three seasons before disbanding.

There were also strong Black teams in several other cities, such as the Atlantic City Vandals; the Independent Pleasure Club from Orange, New Jersey; the Philadelphia Panthers; and the Monticello Athletic Association of Pittsburgh, led by five-foot-four guard Cumberland Posey. Posey was an ace long-range shooter in the days of layups and five-foot shots and was considered the best player of his

Smart Set Athletic Club basketball team, 1900s

day—Black or white. In one game, Posey, who also played professional baseball, scored fifteen points and drained a twenty-foot shot to clinch a 24-to-19 win against defending champs Howard University. He went on to become one of the first sports moguls, playing for and then owning a baseball team called the Homestead Grays in the Negro Leagues. In fact, Posey is the only inductee in both the Baseball *and* Basketball Halls of Fame.

For the latter part of the 1910s, most teams remained amateur and played only for the sport of it, primarily representing athletic clubs, churches, schools, neighborhoods, local businesses, and social organizations. But that would soon change.

After the end of World War I, America strode into the 1920s with a new brand of confidence and an even bolder sense of style. The stock market was booming, and the country was prosperous. Uptown in New York City, new artistic voices were emerging. Great writers like James Weldon Johnson and Zora Neale Hurston, musicians like Duke Ellington and Ethel Waters, painters like Aaron Douglas, actors like Paul Robeson, and athletes like Joe Louis were blossoming in the city's Black mecca. Harlem was fat and sassy, and the world would soon find out about her new basketball team that was taking the game by storm.

THE NEW YORK RENAISSANCE

"It was the Rens, not the Knicks, who brought home New York City's first official pro basketball title."

—John Isaacs, New York Renaissance Big Five

In 1923, an amateur team from Manhattan named the Spartan Braves was rechristened the New York Renaissance Big Five by former player turned owner Bob Douglas, a straight-backed West Indian fellow from St. Kitts. He named the team after the Harlem Renaissance Casino, where they played their home games. The premier Black basketball team in the country, the Renaissance Big Five attracted some of the best athletic talent, like sharpshooting William "Pop" Gates; Charles "Tarzan" Cooper, a dominant center and rebounder; Zack Clayton, a brilliant multisport athlete; and scoring power forward George Crowe.

The Harlem Rens, as the team became known, played straight-up, no-nonsense basketball: suffocating defense, sharp quick passes, a fast-breaking offense. They kept the ball on the move, off the floor,

Harlem Rens home game in the Renaissance Casino's ballroom, 1920s

R
NEW 4

and ahead of the man. The players were in great condition and ran and passed all night long, whipping the ball up and down the court so fast the ball would practically hum. "Keep it off your wrist!" they'd say. "Give and go!" "Treat it like a hot potato!" They were like a jazz quintet—fluid, improvisational, harmonic—every player in tune, shining individually, and even more beautifully together. The Rens always brought the house down. It was basketball at its finest.

And let me tell you something: Home games at the Renaissance Casino were high-class affairs not to be missed! Folks showed up in their Sunday best, just wanting to be seen in their stylish threads. There was always a fancy dinner in the ballroom before the game. And when it was game time, they cleared the dance floor and wheeled out tall baskets. The court was small and a little slippery, but it didn't matter—the Rens made quick work of the visiting team. When the game was over, the baskets were removed, and a swing band came out so folks could dance the night away. And let me tell you something else: *Everybody* played the Renaissance. Ella Fitzgerald, Chick Webb, Duke Ellington, Count Basie, Earl "Fatha" Hines—they were all down there. Jamming, showing the people a good time.

The Rens' away games weren't quite as swanky. Unlike professional baseball's Negro Leagues, there was no major league for African American basketball players back then. The Rens spent most of their season on the road, barnstorming in big and small towns between New York and Chicago as well as across the Midwest to Kansas City, St. Louis, and Milwaukee, and into Minnesota. They played every day of the week and even twice on Sundays, winning about nine times out of ten. One year, they even had an eighty-eight-game winning streak. They traveled anywhere from one hundred to three hundred miles a day in their own bus, which they called the Blue Goose. It seated ten people. The guys snacked on salami and crackers, played cards, and harmonized their way down highways and country back roads. In some towns, they had to go a hundred miles or so out of their way to find a place to sleep, 'cause Black folks weren't welcome everywhere. Most of their games were played against white competition in nonleague games billed as exhibitions. They drew large crowds against teams like the Philadelphia Sphas and the Indianapolis Kautskys. A popular matchup was between the Rens and the Original Celtics. The Rens' fast-paced, fluid style was great competition for the Celtics' solid skill set. Their games sometimes drew as many as fifteen thousand fans, and the Rens beat the Celtics about as often as they lost to them. Over the years, players from both teams became good friends and came to respect each other. They all knew that their matches guaranteed nice paydays for everyone.

Harlem Globetrotters barnstorming game, 1920s

THE HARLEM GLOBETROTTERS

"In the very beginning, I didn't know anything about the Celtics, the Knicks, or any of them. I knew only about the Harlem Globetrotters."

—Kareem Abdul-Jabbar, Los Angeles Lakers

In 1927, as the Rens were enjoying their success, another Black team came along and changed the game of basketball. They were from Chicago and made up of some of the original members of the Savoy Big Five, an amateur Black team that played its home games at the Savoy Ballroom in Chicago. Their new promoter and owner, Abe Saperstein, gave them the name Harlem Globetrotters so that the small-town competition they played on the road would know they were a team of Black players. In those days, it was best to avoid any surprises; otherwise there could be trouble, like having a game canceled or an altercation, or even worse, being run out of town by an angry mob.

During the 1920s and '30s, the Trotters played almost every day of the week, visiting remote parts of the country that were hungry for entertainment. In the team's early years, they played straightforward basketball and rarely lost a game. By the 1930s, the Trotters became such a strong team that they often built big leads against hometown competition, and instead of continuing to run up the score, they would start performing sleight-of-hand tricks with the basketball, known as peppering, and pass it around in a three-man weave for the rest of the game, shooting sparingly. They were careful not to embarrass the local team by blowing them out, because they wanted to be invited back for another game down the road. The crowds loved it. The Trotters even created a pregame warm-up routine called the Magic Circle, where they huddled together on their side of the court and charmed the crowd by spinning the ball on their fingers and making complicated, tricky passes to one another that were altogether captivating. They did it all to the jazzy whistling tune "Sweet Georgia Brown" by Brother Bones that played over the loudspeaker. It eventually became their theme song. From then on, these hijinks became a permanent part of their act, a unique combination of comedy and basketball.

Some Black folks had mixed feelings about the Globetrotters. Many were concerned that the Trotters' goofing around would reinforce the painful stereotype of the "happy Negro" that was a shameful part of many Hollywood films and vaudeville acts back then. Most of the Trotters' spectators were white, after all. But, on the other hand, there was no arguing the fact that the Trotters were supremely talented basketball players. Their no-look passes, half-court hook shots that went in like clockwork,

Reece "Goose" Tatum of the Harlem Globetrotters, the original "Clown Prince of Basketball"

ORIGINAL
HARLEM

and slam dunks weren't yet commonplace in basketball. It was incredible how good they were. Opposing teams would try really hard to win, but they were the ones who usually ended up looking foolish.

The Trotters had a fellow named Marques Haynes—the best ball handler in the world. He would dribble around the court as if the ball were a yo-yo, go down on one knee, then slide on his hip as fast as lightning, all while still dribbling as defenders tried in vain to catch him. They also had a guy by the name of Reece "Goose" Tatum, who played baseball in the Negro Leagues during the summer but was a great basketball player, too. He had the longest arms you will ever see on a human being, with huge hands that worked like big suction cups when he palmed the ball. Every game, he'd pretend to shoot and then he'd just hold on to the ball, making defenders spin like tops as they searched for it. Or sometimes he'd attach an elastic cord to the ball while he shot free throws. The guys in the blocks would all jump at once when the ball went up, only to watch it snap back into Goose's hands. It was hard not to chuckle at that. At some point during every game, he'd bring out a bucket filled with water and chase one of the players around the court, threatening to douse him. When he chucked it, the player would dodge, leaving the referee standing behind him to get soaked, much to the crowd's delight. Later in the game, Goose would come out with another bucket and chase the same player into the crowd. This time when he swung the bucket, the fans would be doused with confetti. It was a guaranteed laugh. Goose kept everybody on their toes.

You might not know it, but the Globetrotters attracted some of the biggest crowds in basketball

history. During their heyday in the 1930s and '40s, they'd bring anywhere from ten thousand to fifty thousand fans to a single game. They were such a good draw that the white leagues would ask them to play the first part of a doubleheader to get fans into the seats. They had whole stadiums in tears with their routine and kids all over the country trying to copy their moves. The Globetrotters spread the gospel of basketball wherever they went.

THE SHOWDOWN

For years, there was a question of who was better, the Rens or the Globetrotters. At the very first World's Championship of Professional Basketball tournament in Chicago, in 1939, the two teams finally met to settle the matter. In front of a packed crowd, the Rens defeated the Globetrotters by a score of 27 to 23. The Rens went on to win the tournament by beating the all-white Oshkosh All Stars from the National Basketball League. That year, the Harlem Rens were the best basketball team in the world. They brought home New York City's first official pro basketball championship. But very few people heard about it: Because the title was won by an African American basketball team, the story wasn't covered in the major papers. The following year, the Trotters and the Rens met again in the tournament. This time the Trotters beat the Rens by a score of 37 to 36 and went on to claim the world championship.

Harlem Rens, Harlem Globetrotters, and owners Bob Douglas and Abe Saperstein, 1939

SECOND QUARTER

The Birth of the NBA

"All those things you read about Jackie Robinson, the abuse, the name-calling… they're all true. I got the same treatment and even worse….It was rough but worth it."

—Harry "Bucky" Lew, Pawtucketville Athletic Club

In 1902, an eighteen-year-old African American fellow named Harry "Bucky" Lew was signed by the Pawtucketville Athletic Club, a previously all-white professional team in Lowell, Massachusetts, that played in the New England Basketball League. Lew had spent the previous years playing at the Lowell YMCA, and he'd developed a reputation for being the best "double dribbler" in the game (it was allowed then). Some of the local papers put pressure on the Pawtucketville Athletic Club to give Bucky a chance to play. Because of injuries, the team took him on as an extra man. In a game against Marlborough on November 6, a starter got injured, leaving the team with only four players against five. At first the manager refused to send Lew into the game, but the crowd grew so angry that it was just about on the verge of a riot. Finally, Bucky went in, becoming the first Black player in professional basketball. He took his lumps and elbows but did well. Bucky Lew continued to play professionally, often barnstorming around New England, for the next twenty years. A few other African American athletes played on otherwise all-white teams—including Frank "Ditto" Wilson for a Fort Plain, New York, team and Hank Williams for the Buffalo Bisons—but by and large, pro basketball remained segregated until the United States entered World War II.

In 1942, large numbers of young American men were going into the military, which caused a shortage of talent for pro basketball. For the first time, white team owners reached across the aisle, and in

Earl Lloyd (second from left) and the NBA's Washington Capitols, 1951

one fell swoop, ten African American players were signed to play in the National Basketball League: Al Price, Casey Jones, Bill Jones, and Shannie Barnett for the Toledo Jim White Chevrolets, and Bernie Price, Roscoe "Duke" Cumberland, Hillery Brown, Tony Peyton, Roosevelt Hudson, and Wyatt "Sonny" Boswell for the Chicago Studebaker Flyers. They took the floor with their white teammates at the start of the 1942–43 season. It was a huge step for basketball—indeed, a huge step for *all* professional sports. Unfortunately, almost no one paid attention or wrote about it in the press. Basketball still had a *long* way to go before it became a major American sport. Pro basketball stood a distant fifth place behind the much more popular Major League Baseball, pro football, ice hockey, and even college basketball.

It wasn't an easy road for the new members of the league. In some towns, fans spat racial venom at Black players and threw trash on the floor, and in other places, Black folks were not even allowed on the court or opposing teams simply canceled the game. Black players couldn't enjoy meals in restaurants with their teammates or stay with them in white-owned hotels. Hotel clerks told coaches things like "We don't accept blacks" right in front of them. They were forced to eat and sleep on the team bus or find other places to stay. By season's end, it was clear that white professional basketball wasn't yet ready to share the floor with African Americans. None of the Black players returned to the league the next year. Integration had to wait.

The men's professional game in the late 1940s was still very rough around the edges. Fistfights remained common, and sometimes even the coaches and refs got into it. Elbowing, holding, and outright punching were accepted as part of the game. The owners didn't mind, because they thought a rough-and-tumble sport was what the fans were paying to see.

Games were now played at ice hockey arenas, often in sketchy parts of town most fans didn't want to walk through. The arenas were freezing cold. Fans had to bring coats and blankets, and if players weren't starting, they draped themselves with towels and huddled on the bench next to space heaters to keep warm. The wooden floor was assembled right on top of the ice, and if the insulation wasn't right, water leaked to the surface, making slick spots. Guys were slipping and sliding all over the place. Sometimes, the ref tossed up the ball for the opening tip-off and almost all the players went down. By halftime, a cloud of evaporated water and cigar smoke hung over the court, making it hard to see the action.

Some courts, like the Boston Garden, had really bad dead spots, too, where the ball wouldn't bounce so well. The smart players knew where they were and stole the ball when opponents dribbled over them.

Al Price, Casey Jones, Bill Jones, and Shannie Barnett of the NBL's Toledo Jim White Chevrolets, 1940s

TOLEDO
63
TOLEDO
55
TOLEDO
52

Other courts were hard as concrete, and back then, everybody wore canvas sneakers with rubber soles that had virtually no padding or support. Over time, those courts did a number on your feet, knees, and back. There were also back-to-back games and an awful lot of traveling, so getting a good night's rest was tough. Players weren't always able to wash their uniforms regularly, and that made for some really foul-smelling bus rides between games, let me tell you.

After World War II ended in 1945, millions of returning American soldiers and a growing economy helped boost attendance at professional basketball games. This in turn made white team owners more willing to try integration again. It also helped that, in 1947, Jackie Robinson broke the color barrier in Major League Baseball when he played with the Brooklyn Dodgers, demonstrating that Black and white athletes could play together at the highest level. That same year, a few African American basketball players could be found in the NBL: William "Dolly" King, a multisport professional athlete with the Rochester Royals; Pop Gates with the Tri-Cities Blackhawks; Willie King with the Detroit Gems; and Bill Farrow with the Youngstown Bears.

But a bolder move was needed. In 1948, Abe Saperstein, the owner of the Globetrotters, challenged the all-white Minneapolis Lakers, defending champions of the National Basketball League, to a single-game showdown to determine which one was the top team in the country.

The Lakers were led by the NBL's biggest draw and best player, George Mikan, a six-foot-ten, 245-pound bespectacled giant from Joliet, Illinois. In the early days of basketball, the average player was between five-eight and five-ten. Anyone approaching six-foot-five or taller was considered to be ungainly, sluggish, and uncoordinated. Mikan was the game's first dominant big man, and unlike his predecessors, he could move. He was virtually unstoppable in the paint, and he had what we called "educated elbows." He could draw a foul and had a wide array of shots, but he primarily relied on a deadly hook shot that he could sink with either hand. He was particularly lethal on the offensive boards and was a shot-blocking machine—even swatting away shots directly over the rim. He was so effective that, by his junior year of college in 1944–45, the NCAA had banned the practice, which they labeled "goaltending," a rule also adopted by the NBL that season. To contain big men like Mikan, the pros would eventually widen the lane from six feet to twelve feet, making players stand farther away from the basket to avoid a three-second violation for camping out in the paint. But these changes didn't stop Mikan from dominating the game. According to the sporting public, and thanks to Mikan, the Lakers were the best basketball team around.

George Mikan of the Minneapolis Lakers

LAKERS

But Abe knew his Globetrotters were on the same level, and when the mighty Lakers accepted the challenge, fans all over the country sat up and paid attention.

The historic contest took place on February 19, 1948. From the opening tip-off, the two teams battled hard. There were no fancy tricks or peppering. It was straight-up basketball for forty minutes. With the game tied in the last quarter at 59 to 59 and only a few seconds left on the clock, the Trotters' Ermer Robinson tossed up a twenty-foot jump shot. He buried it. The buzzer sounded, and over seventeen thousand fans jumped out of their seats. The Trotters won the game by a single basket, proving that Black players could play the game at the same level as the white pros. Sometimes, even better.

The NBL, suffering slow ticket sales, staggered through the 1948–49 season and was nearly sunk when four of its teams, including the Minneapolis Lakers, jumped ship to the Basketball Association of America (BAA), which had started two years earlier. The remaining NBL teams invited Bob Douglas and his New York Renaissance to replace a losing team that had recently folded. The Rens joined the league in the middle of the season, becoming the first all-Black team to play in a major professional basketball league. Douglas moved the team to Dayton, Ohio, renamed them the Dayton Rens, and tried his best to make a go of it. Unfortunately, the Rens didn't fare so well. Joining a league six weeks into the season and inheriting a 2–17 record, let alone moving to an all-white Midwestern town that wasn't ready for them, was tough for the players. Neither the players nor the fans had time to adjust, and the Rens ended up with a losing record.

The 1948–49 season would be the last one for the NBL and the BAA. On August 3, 1949, they merged to form a new league: the National Basketball Association (NBA). The NBA began its season with seventeen teams, including the Boston Celtics, the New York Knickerbockers, the Syracuse Nationals, and the Chicago Stags. The brand-new league agreed that it would not welcome African American teams or players. Douglas's Dayton Rens were left out of the merger, and the ten Black players in the league were cut loose. It spelled the end for the mighty Rens as a team. They were later acquired by the Globetrotters, which by then had multiple teams playing around the country and overseas.

The NBA played its first season in 1949–50 and struggled. To increase attendance, the league invited one of the Globetrotter teams to play the first game of a doubleheader. Since the Trotters were a hot ticket, they packed the house. But when their game ended, half the people in the stands got up and left. It gave the all-white owners something to think about. By this time, the

Nat "Sweetwater" Clifton of the Harlem Globetrotters tips off against George Mikan of the Minneapolis Lakers

Trotters were consistently playing in front of sold-out crowds around the country, and the NBA couldn't get enough fans to come to its own arenas.

It took only a single season for the owners to realize that Jim Crow basketball was hurting their bottom line. The NBA integrated the following season, signing four African American players: Chuck Cooper, who was drafted out of Duquesne University in Pittsburgh; Hank DeZonie from the Saratoga Harlem Yankees; Nat "Sweetwater" Clifton from the Globetrotters; and Earl Lloyd, who was drafted out of West Virginia State University. It wasn't exactly a Jackie Robinson moment, though. There had already been numerous African American players in professional basketball, and when the new group of players joined the year-old NBA, they didn't garner much attention in the national papers.

Pro basketball still lagged behind the college game, which had become hugely popular in the 1930s, with yearly double-headers at Madison Square Garden. The tide turned only when a college basketball point-shaving scandal broke out in the early 1950s and the public lost trust in the "pure" game college ball was supposed to offer. After that, fans began to pay attention to the pros.

There was also a new kid in the league who played the game like no one had ever seen in the NBA. He grew up playing pickup basketball in a St. Albans schoolyard in New York City and toured with the Harlem Globetrotters as a college standout. At a time when most players played a deliberate, fundamental style of the game, he defied convention and brought schoolyard flash to the pros. His name was Bob Cousy. Drafted out of Holy Cross in 1950, he was all of six-one and 175 pounds, but he had large hands, long arms that gave him wonderful control of the ball, and great peripheral vision that gave him incredible court awareness. Cooz was the ultimate point guard. He knew just where every player was on the fast break and how and where to get the ball to him. His signature moves were behind-the-back dribbles and no-look passes. By the mid-1950s, Bob Cousy was the best and most popular athlete in professional basketball. Sportswriters called him Mr. Basketball. His brilliant style breathed new life into the Boston Celtics and the entire league after George Mikan retired in 1956. Cooz was a glimpse into the future of modern basketball.

Throughout the 1950s, there was a slow trickle of African American players into the league. An unwritten quota limited the number of Black players allowed per team to *one or two*. They also weren't given much opportunity to play to their full potential. Most of them were used primarily as role players—rebounders, defenders, or passers who set up their white teammates to score—so there weren't any standouts in the group, nor did they have much impact on the game. Pro basketball remained flat and uninteresting, and fans stayed away. If the game was going to capture the attention of the country, it needed to clear the lane for a new crop of youngsters who would break the old rules. By the beginning of the 1960s, when Black folks were also making progress in other aspects of American life thanks to the Civil Rights Movement, the revolutionaries of basketball were on their way.

Bob Cousy of the Boston Celtics

HALFTIME

From the Playground to the Pros

THE SCHOOLYARD

"My game really takes off on the playgrounds." —Julius Erving, New York Nets

Unlike baseball and football, basketball doesn't require any expensive equipment. All you need are a ball and some sneakers. When the game leaped out of indoor gymnasiums and onto outdoor playgrounds, basketball exploded in urban areas. In 1933, there were about one hundred outdoor basketball courts in New York City. By 1960, the number had grown to almost two thousand.

To this day, some of the best basketball in the world can be found on the blacktops of small towns in the South and Midwest and in large cities like New York, Chicago, and Washington, DC. Many of the biggest legends of the sport learned and honed their craft by playing pickup basketball on outdoor courts and in gymnasiums: Bob Cousy, Oscar Robertson, Elgin Baylor, Julius Erving, Connie Hawkins, Kareem Abdul-Jabbar, Michael Jordan, and Earl Manigault among them. Pickup basketball is sacred. It is gritty, physical, and full of swagger and trash-talking. Only the strongest survive. Winners stay on; losers sit and wait for the next game. Basketball skills and bragging rights are the currency.

The aggressive and showy "hot dog" style of the playground game wasn't welcome in buttoned-up college and pro ball. The owners and coaches of organized teams preferred to stick to mechanical, by-the-book basketball that didn't allow for much individual flair. It worked for college ball, where players were still learning how to play the fundamental team game. But pro ball was a different matter. Putting butts in the seats was the name of the game, and by the late 1960s, it was time to introduce a new brand of play that would take the game to the next level.

Connie Hawkins dunks during a New York City street basketball game, 1960s

THE ABA: THE OTHER LEAGUE

"We were ahead of the NBA in so many different ways. We had the 3-point play.... We used pressing and trapping defenses....We had All-Star weekends, Slam Dunk Contests, and we even had the best officials."

—Hubie Brown, Kentucky Colonels head coach

"It was a crazy league. No doubt about it." —Rick Barry, Oakland Oaks

In the summer of 1967, the NBA discovered it was no longer the only game in town. A group of basketball-crazy businessmen and investors got together to form a new professional basketball league called the American Basketball Association (ABA). They hired NBA vet George Mikan to head it, established eleven teams, and were off and running. Their main goal was to create a competitive league and ultimately force a merger with the NBA.

To distinguish their league from the NBA, the ABA introduced a new red-white-and-blue basketball and assembled rosters that were, shall we say, unconventional. Either the players couldn't play in the NBA for some reason, or they were willing to leave college earlier than the NBA would take them, or they were ready to play straight out of high school. The ABA also lured a few players away from the NBA, forcing the old guard to take notice.

The ABA was untraditional in other ways, too. Its player demographics were very different compared with the NBA's: primarily African American with relatively few white players. And the owners were willing to do whatever it took to promote their games. They had dancing cheerleaders at halftime, costumed mascots throwing giveaways into the crowd, cow-milking contests, alligator wrestling, hot-dog-eating contests, free pizza nights, free basketball nights, free T-shirt nights, and free burger nights. You name it, they had it. It was nuts.

The ABA courts also had a three-point line. The NCAA had tried out the three-point goal for a single game in 1945, and it was used for a while in the short-lived American Basketball League, but it never caught on. Despite that fact, the ABA embraced the three-point shot and made it popular. The new rule allowed shorter players to become offensive threats outside the key, and it forced defenders to move farther away from the basket. As players spread out more on the floor, the middle opened up for driving layups. Every time the ball fell through the hoop from twenty-two feet away, it was as though

Julius Erving of the New York Nets glides over opposing players from the Spirits of St. Louis, 1975

NETS
32
Spirits St. Louis
Spirits St. Louis
NETS
22
NETS
24
Spirits St. Louis
1

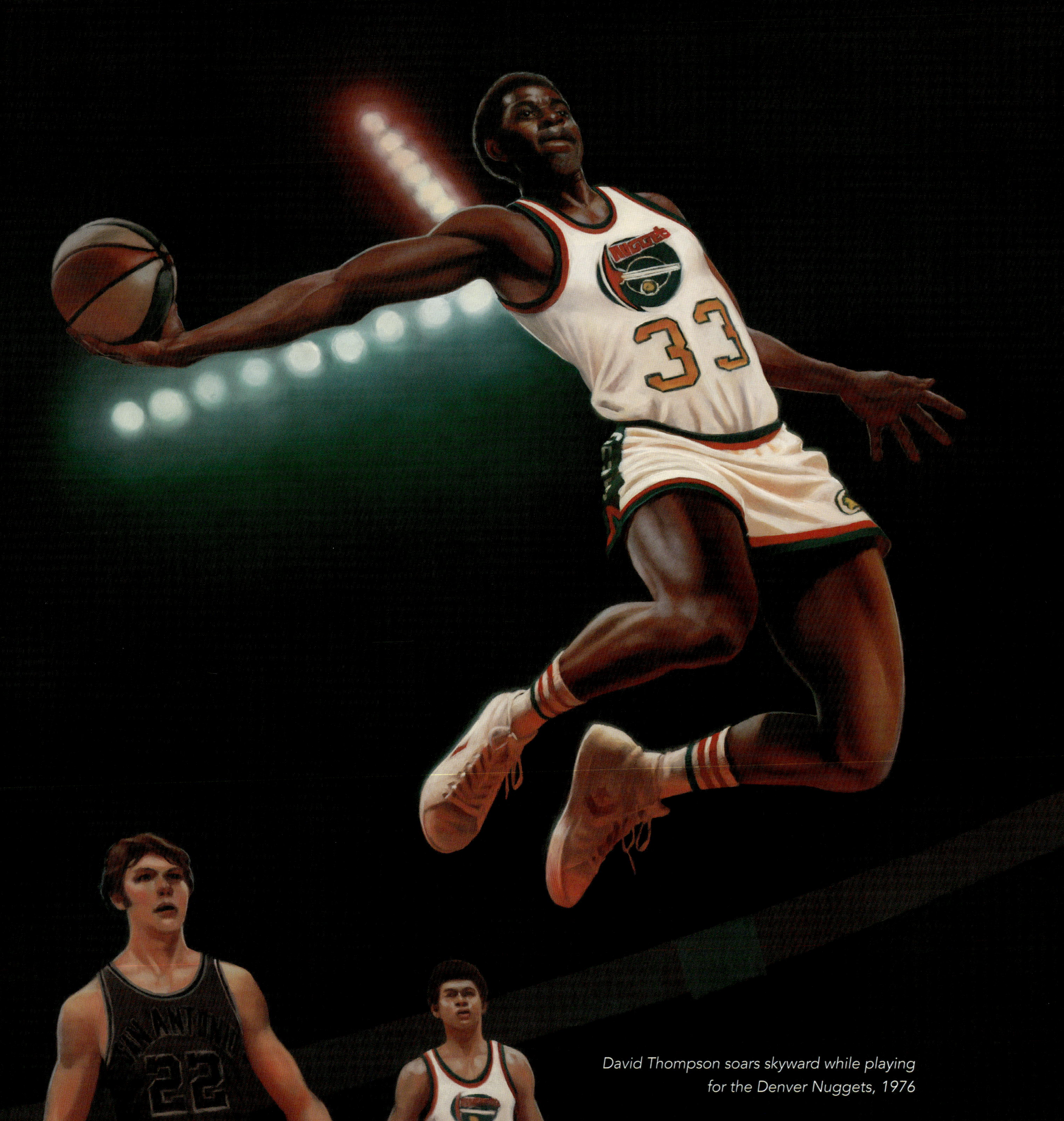

David Thompson soars skyward while playing for the Denver Nuggets, 1976

a dagger had been plunged into the heart of the opposing team. It was as exciting as a home run in baseball, and the crowds went wild.

There weren't many set plays in the ABA, though. Their games were fast and loose, heavy on the slam dunks and light on the defense, and the scores were high, often in the 110s and higher. It was an exciting combination of schoolyard swagger and highly skilled professional basketball. The stuff the players were doing was incredible. They had this dude named David Thompson who could leap like he was taking off from a trampoline. His game was all the way above the rim, and he had a sweet jump shot, too. Some credit him with popularizing the alley-oop, where an offensive player jumps and catches a pass thrown near the rim and then slam-dunks or taps the ball into the basket before returning to the ground. Rick Barry, who jumped ship from the NBA, was a solid small forward with all-around skills—pure hustle and a scoring machine. Then there was George "Iceman" Gervin. His game was smooth. He made an art form of the finger-roll layup, a move where a player shoots the ball underhand with either hand, letting the ball roll off the fingertips to arc into the basket without touching the backboard. And Moses Malone, Connie Hawkins, Dan Issel, Artis Gilmore—there were so many. The biggest draw in the league was Julius Erving, whom everybody called the Doctor. When he got the ball, he'd wrap his big hands around it, leap into the air, and throw it down into the hoop with power and style. Julius tore the roof off many a stadium.

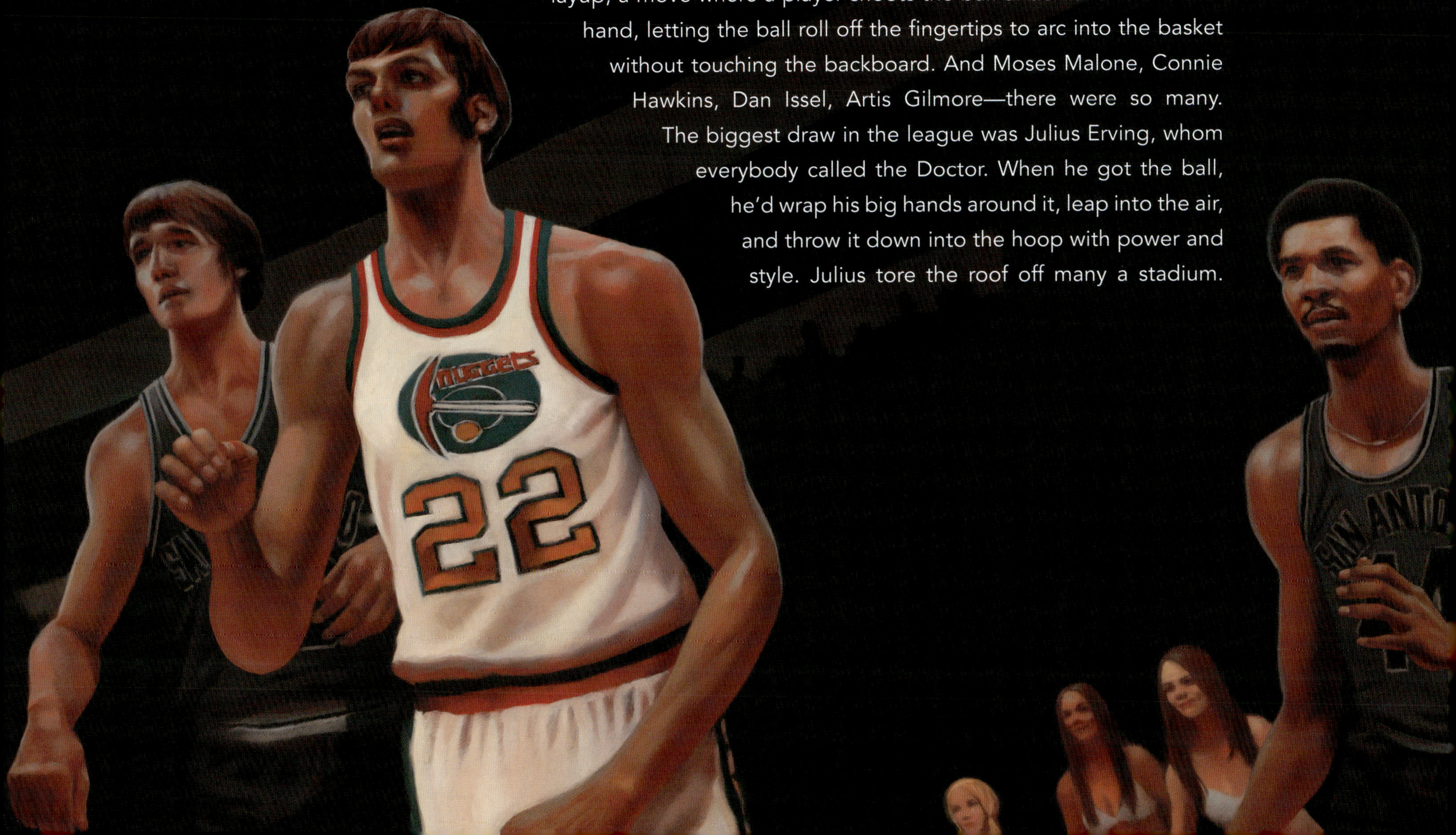

Colonels
10
PONY

He was the league's premier ambassador. Another incredible player was Marvin "Bad News" Barnes, but he wasn't exactly the most reliable fellow in the league. He was hot-blooded and not shy about using his fists. In fact, fighting was a big issue all across the ABA. There was a brawl in just about *every* game. Those guys were a rough bunch. Some of them even kept guns in their lockers.

Fans showed up to ABA games well before tip-off to watch the teams warm up. During layup drills, the players often made these incredible slam dunks, getting more creative with each one. The fans loved it. In fact, it's where the idea for the slam dunk contest came from. During the 1976 ABA All-Star Game in Denver, Colorado, they had the world's first official slam dunk competition at halftime. There were six guys in the competition, including the league's highest flyers, Julius Erving and David Thompson. David Thompson led with an awesome 360-degree slam dunk that made the fans jump out of their seats. It seemed like he'd take the prize. But, man, it was Dr. J who brought the house down with a soaring slam dunk, taking off from the free-throw line. Nobody had *ever* seen that before.

A lot of the guys say the best thing about the ABA was the players, and it's true. The ABA was where the most exciting professional basketball was being played at the time. It was playground basketball at the highest level. Problem was, nobody outside the stadiums was watching. Attendance was low across the league, and games weren't shown on television, so very few people got to see the incredible feats of Julius Erving, Connie Hawkins, Moses Malone, Rick Barry, George Gervin, and all the other talented players. Poor ticket sales forced several teams to move to different cities from year to year, or fold altogether. By the league's eighth year, it was on its last legs. At the end of the 1976 season, only seven of the eleven ABA teams were still in business—not enough to play another full season. Although the ABA had the most exciting players, it needed a larger stage, a more solid and organized foundation. It needed the NBA.

That summer, four of the seven remaining ABA teams were absorbed by the NBA: the San Antonio Spurs, New York Nets, Denver Nuggets, and Indiana Pacers. The other three teams were either paid off or disbanded. The NBA soon adopted the three-point line, the slam dunk competition, and many of the ABA's crazy promotional tactics, such as giveaways and dancing cheerleaders. At last, the world got to see what it had been missing all those years. Pro basketball got a second wind, a brand-new exciting style that combined fundamental basketball, incredible athleticism, brash individualism, and playground swagger. It was classical music, jazz, hip-hop, and rock and roll all rolled up together—a beautiful combination. The age of modern basketball had arrived.

Louie Dampier of the Kentucky Colonels launches a three-pointer, 1975

BULLS
23
BULLS
54
NEW YORK
2
BULLS
KNICKS

THIRD QUARTER

The Revolutionaries

"Everybody in the NBA is good. And then you have the really good ones and the great ones."

—Kyrie Irving, Cleveland Cavaliers

The game of basketball has produced some of the greatest athletes the world has ever seen. Remarkably talented scorers, defenders, ball handlers, shot blockers, and playmakers whose world-class athleticism, razor-sharp wits, and unique playing styles lifted them to the top of the sport.

Among the all-time list of supremely talented basketball players is an elite group of innovators whose contributions proved so important that they became essential components of the game, influencing every player who followed. These basketball juggernauts stretched boundaries, elevating and fine-tuning gameplay, making it more exciting, more competitive, and more challenging. Each is among the very best of his era. They did what great players do—they changed the game.

You've already heard about Cumberland Posey, one of basketball's first and most-skilled long-range gunners; Hank Luisetti, Glenn Roberts, and Jumpin' Joe Fulks, some of the first jump shooters; George Mikan, the game's first agile and versatile big man; Bob Cousy, the NBA's premier tricky point guard; and Goose Tatum and the Harlem Globetrotters, whose clever and humorous antics saved the NBA from going under. There's also David Thompson, one of the ABA's greatest leapers and slam dunk contest originators, and George Gervin, who dazzled the league with his smooth finger-roll layups. They were some of the best ever to play the game, but there have been even more masterful practitioners whose magnificent improvements have taken the sport to new heights.

One of these pioneers was a towering center from the deep South who terrified jump shooters all over the league with his innovative and intimidating defense.

Michael Jordan of the Chicago Bulls soars for a slam dunk against the New York Knicks at Madison Square Garden, 1993

CELTICS
6

BILL RUSSELL

"I had never seen a blocked shot in a basketball game before I did it!"

—Bill Russell, Boston Celtics

Bill Russell was the first of a new generation of players who turned the game upside down. Before the mid-1950s, coaches insisted that defenders always keep their feet on the floor. "Don't leave your feet, or they'll dribble right into you and draw the foul." That made sense for some players, but when it came to Bill Russell, he went his own way.

Bill was a lean and muscular six-foot-ten, 220-pound center from Monroe, Louisiana. He played college ball at the University of San Francisco, where he led his team to an undefeated season and two national championships. The following summer he snapped up an Olympic gold medal before playing his rookie season with the Boston Celtics, where he would spend his entire thirteen-year career. When Russell broke into pro ball in 1956, he shattered the mold. Tall, quick, and strong, he had great leaping ability. Unlike his predecessors, who stayed on the ground while playing defense, Russell took to the air to block shots. He became a master at it, terrorizing shooting guards, forwards, and centers all across the league, leaping high, often just tapping the ball to the point guard on the perimeter, who was already in motion, heading toward the other end of the court for an easy score. Russell's philosophy was *Why slap it out of bounds when you can keep possession of the ball?* Players thought twice about taking shots anywhere in his vicinity. His strategy was psychological. He would impose his will on every play, controlling the tempo by blocking shots early and continuing to dominate the paint until the final buzzer sounded.

He wasn't a big scorer, but he didn't need to be—his defense was his offense. Russell was a supreme student of the game, closely scrutinizing his teammates and opponents to find their strengths and weaknesses, and then exploiting them with precision. He was a solid passer, too. He always put his team first and took great pride in elevating the play of all his teammates. Russell helped lead the Boston Celtics to multiple championships and even became a player-coach toward the end of his career—the first African American coach in the NBA. I'll put it this way: Before Russell joined Boston, the Celtics were a winning team. But after he joined the team, they became a dynasty. He was the missing piece. Russell has more championship rings than any other basketball player. Eleven in all. Bill Russell showed the world that big men didn't have to be lumbering giants. Big men can jump.

Bill Russell

PHILA
13

WILT CHAMBERLAIN

"[I'm] the villain of the NBA, the superstar you love to hate."

—Wilt Chamberlain, Los Angeles Lakers

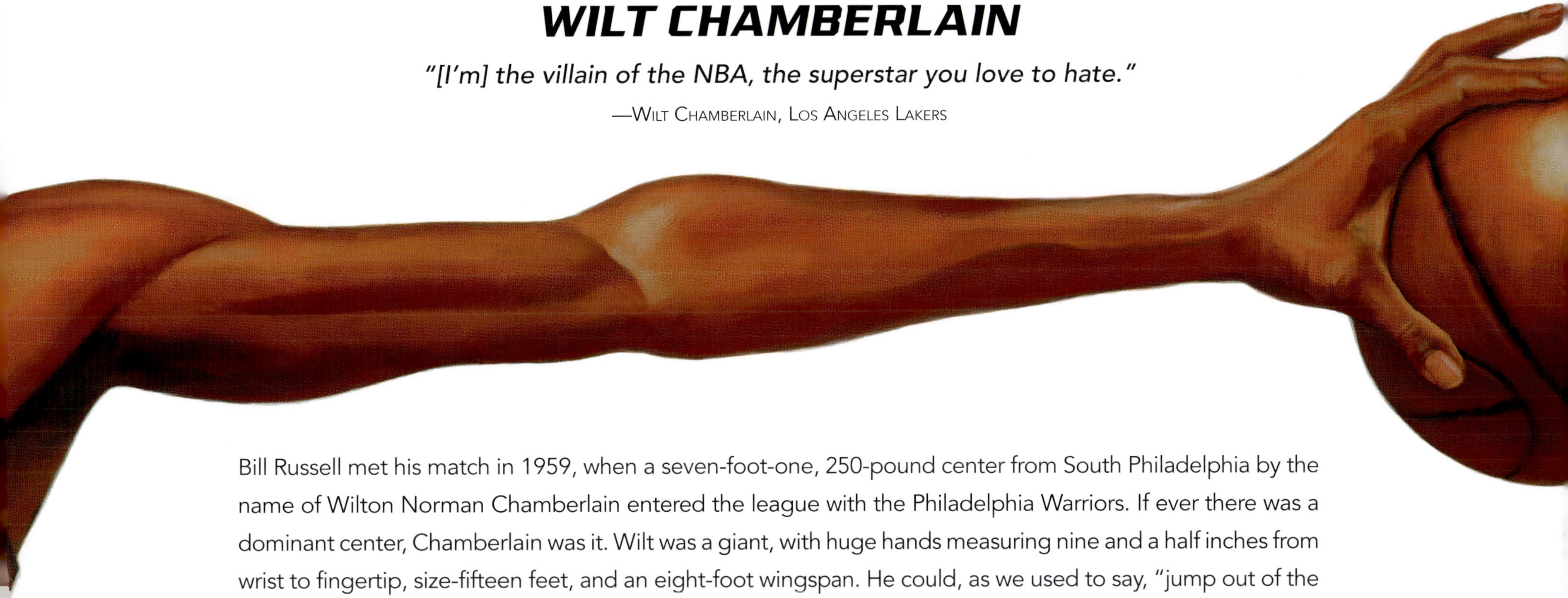

Bill Russell met his match in 1959, when a seven-foot-one, 250-pound center from South Philadelphia by the name of Wilton Norman Chamberlain entered the league with the Philadelphia Warriors. If ever there was a dominant center, Chamberlain was it. Wilt was a giant, with huge hands measuring nine and a half inches from wrist to fingertip, size-fifteen feet, and an eight-foot wingspan. He could, as we used to say, "jump out of the gym" and run the forty-yard dash in under five seconds. They called him the Big Dipper because he had to dip under doorways when entering a room. Dip could grab the net with both hands from a standing position. And even though he was as tall as a tree and as strong as an ox, Wilt had a soft shooting touch. He had a nice fallaway shot, too, where he would jump and shoot as he was drifting backward, away from the basket.

Wilt was a scorer. In high school, he scored ninety points in one game and seventy-four in another. In the pros, he averaged fifty points per game for a full season, and he even once scored one hundred points in a single game—the most by any professional player ever. Opposing teams sent two or three guys at once to try and guard him. But Wilt was unstoppable. He owned the boards, blocked shots from all sides, led the league in scoring and assists, and dunked on just about everybody. When Wilt was coming at you, you just had to get out of his way. It was pretty much an unfair situation.

Because of Wilt, the league widened the lane from twelve to sixteen feet, banned offensive goaltending and over-the-backboard inbound passes (Wilt would catch them over players' heads and score), and revised the rules for free-throw shooting (Wilt would leap from behind the foul line to make a basket)—just to make it fairer for everybody else. Didn't matter, though. Wilt still dominated.

Wilt Chamberlain

JERRY WEST

"I loved hearing the clock go down. Five, four, three, two, one, and then letting [the ball] go....I lived for that."

—Jerry West, Los Angeles Lakers

One year after Wilt made his debut, a talented young rookie from Chelyan, West Virginia, joined the league with the Los Angeles Lakers. His name was Jerry West. He stood at only six-two and weighed a mere 185 pounds, relatively small for a basketball player, but West made up for it with strong fundamentals, relentless hustle, and unshakable confidence. He was without question one of the most intense players in the game, giving everything he had on the floor and never taking a second off.

His practice habits were extreme. He shot the ball hundreds of times per day, until his fingers bled, and worked himself into excellent condition. He made basketball his religion, the court his temple, and he aimed squarely for pure perfection. Jerry believed that every time the ball left his hands it would go through the net. He developed a trademark quick-release jump shot that was very hard to block. He once had a close-to-perfect game, making sixteen of seventeen shots from the floor and twelve of twelve free throws, with twelve assists and ten blocked shots. He was tough as nails, too. He played through injuries and broke his nose at least nine times over his career. If you were down by a bucket with only a few seconds left on the clock, he was the man you trusted with the ball. He lived for that moment. More often than not, he'd bury it, too, which is why we called him Mr. Clutch. He was a great individual player and an even greater team player. Everybody liked Jerry. He was the face of the league. Literally. He's the guy on the NBA logo, for goodness' sake.

Jerry West

LAKERS

OSCAR ROBERTSON

"My athletic ability, size, skills, and basketball knowledge gave experts a sense of the future."

—Oscar Robertson, Cincinnati Royals

If there's anything to be said about Oscar "the Big O" Robertson, it can be communicated in two words: triple-double—a term used to describe an individual player posting double-digit statistics in three of five categories (points, assists, rebounds, steals, and blocks) during a single game. Robertson was the first player to maintain a triple-double average for a complete season, something akin to hitting over .400 in baseball. Very few people have done it. When Oscar entered the league with the Cincinnati Royals, the young man showed the world what a complete player looked like. He was a master when it came to scoring, rebounding, and making assists, and he routinely lit up scoreboards with a full arsenal of ten-foot jumpers, layups, twenty-foot outside shots, and post-up moves close to the basket.

Robertson was one of the game's first big guards, at six-foot-five and 210 pounds. He bulked up as a youngster by doing farm work over summer breaks in high school, and later he honed his skills by playing pickup basketball at the Dust Bowl, an outdoor park adjacent to the first public-housing projects in Indianapolis, where he grew up. His game wasn't flashy, but Oz could bring it. He dominated the league as a high school standout and put on a show at Madison Square Garden in 1958 as a college player. He did the same in the pros. In his prime, no one could stop the Big O, who was *everywhere*, doing *everything* on the court.

Oscar Robertson

BOUT
ROUND
GO
12
34

ELGIN BAYLOR

"'How many points you gonna score tonight?' came the usual question. 'About 70,' said Baylor."

—Milton Gross, "Elgin Baylor and Basketball's Big Explosion"

There are two eras in basketball history: pre–Elgin Baylor and post–Elgin Baylor. Before Elgin was a rookie in the late 1950s, basketball was played close to the ground. Players had to know what they were going to do with the ball before they left their feet. It was a horizontal game that sometimes went vertical. After Elgin, basketball was played on a diagonal. He was a revolutionary. The man would leap into the air and seem to stay there, then change direction, float past and split defenders, and make midair acrobatic shots or passes that defied gravity.

A Washington, DC, native, Baylor was six-five, 225 pounds, and he played the game like a man possessed, often scoring forty, fifty, sixty, and even seventy-one points in a single game, all without the three-point line. He did it with a unique shooting style of jumping and hanging in the air before releasing the ball, shooting it on the way down instead of on the way up, arcing the ball just high enough to sail over the defender's hand. They called it hang time. It was beautiful. He would dance circles around the defense, scoring at will with reverse layups thrown backward over his head as he glided under the basket. He perfected dazzling passes, yo-yo dribbling, spin moves, and fallaway jumpers, banking the ball in from every angle like a masterful pool player.

Baylor also had the most deceptive dribble and first step in basketball. He had a nervous tic that threw off defenders. Opponents couldn't tell whether he was faking a pass or just doing his thing. Whatever it was, it worked. He averaged 27.4 points per game over his career, and he once dropped sixty-one points in a playoff game against Bill Russell's Celtics, a record that stood for twenty-four years. The man was a beast. He scored forty-nine or more points in a game at least twenty-one times in his career.

Baylor showed the world what basketball looked like when style, hang time, and prolific scoring came together. He helped resuscitate the fledgling Lakers after the team moved to Los Angeles, jump-starting pro basketball on the West Coast, and putting DC playground basketball on the map. He was Michael Jordan before Michael Jordan, Julius Erving before Julius Erving. He was Elgin Baylor, a man ahead of his time.

Elgin Baylor (center)

Los Angeles
NEW

33

KAREEM ABDUL-JABBAR

"When the skyhook is working, the hook and I are one."

—Kareem Abdul-Jabbar, Los Angeles Lakers

In 1965, a lanky seven-foot, eighteen-year-old kid from New York City was the most recruited high school basketball player in the country. Kareem Abdul-Jabbar, who was known as Lew Alcindor before he converted to Islam and changed his name, was highly intelligent, introspective, stoic, soft-spoken, and graceful, and he was dangerous with a basketball. At UCLA, Abdul-Jabbar played under legendary coach John Wooden, whose teams won more NCAA championships than any other college basketball team in history. Kareem dominated, scoring and slam-dunking on all comers and leading his Bruins to three straight championships.

It's because of Abdul-Jabbar that the NCAA banned the slam dunk in 1967 to try to thwart his dominance in the paint. It didn't work. He had another shot up his sleeve, a potent and virtually undefendable weapon: the skyhook. He mastered the shot and made it famous, wielding it his entire basketball career. He would pivot and leap high off one foot, keeping his body between the ball and the defender. As he glided upward, his arm would extend toward the heavens. At the peak of his jump, he'd release the ball with a flick of the wrist and watch it arc beautifully over the defender's outstretched hands, then splash through the net like a plump raindrop. It was ballet on the hardwood. The skyhook worked no matter how tall the defender or how high the defender could jump. No one could reach it.

Armed with his undefendable shot, Abdul-Jabbar led the Milwaukee Bucks to the 1971 NBA championship in his second year in the league, playing alongside newly traded veteran Oscar Robertson. Shortly after the season, Lew Alcindor changed his name to Kareem Abdul-Jabbar, which in Arabic means "noble powerful servant." Indeed. His teammates also called him the Captain. A few years after winning the championship, he was traded to the Lakers, where he eventually teamed up with a rookie named Earvin "Magic" Johnson. Together they won five more championships.

Kareem kept himself in great shape with an intense training regimen and by practicing yoga. He even studied martial arts under Bruce Lee and starred in a few feature films. By the end of his twenty-year career, Abdul-Jabbar had scored more points than anyone in the history of the game, a record that stood for nearly thirty-nine years. Cap retired at the ripe old age of forty-two as one of the greatest ever to play the game.

Kareem Abdul-Jabbar

JULIUS ERVING

"Call me the Doctor." —Julius Erving, Virginia Squires

Julius Erving was a New York City playground legend after he played at Harlem's world-famous Rucker Park. Julius routinely drew large crowds on the uptown blacktop with his amazing athletic feats. Spectators choked the sidelines and bleachers, lined the tops of neighboring buildings and bridges, and even scaled nearby fences and trees to catch a glimpse of the Doctor. And for good reason. Julius did things on the basketball court that weren't even imaginable at the time—literally jumping over defenders to dunk the basketball. They joked that he could jump so high he could grab a dollar from the top of the backboard and leave change. Erving was the very first person to dunk from the free-throw line in an official slam dunk competition. He was an expert rebounder, too, snatching boards with some of the largest hands in the game. The Doctor stood at six-seven, weighed 210 pounds, and when he held a basketball, it looked like it was the size of a volleyball. If he shook hands with an average person, his fingertips went halfway to their elbow.

Julius often tricked defenders by palming the ball and faking a shot, getting them off their feet or looking the other way. He had a sweet jumper and a ridiculous vertical leap. Once, on a fast break when he was with the Philadelphia 76ers, Erving leaped into the air, cupped the ball by pressing it against his forearm, and power-dunked it over the Lakers' Michael Cooper. Another famous shot also happened against the Lakers. Erving jumped from the right side of the key as two defenders leaped up to block him. While in the air, he floated past them, underneath the basket and out of bounds, then, with his right hand, swung the ball back under the backboard to the other side of the rim and kissed it off the glass. Bucket.

Julius took Elgin Baylor–style basketball to the next level. He was one of the greatest leapers ever to play the game, and the classiest dude in basketball. He dressed sharply, drove fancy cars, and could beautifully express his ideas with a smooth delivery. Julius made professional basketball look good.

Julius Erving

MOSES MALONE

"I want the ball." —Moses Malone, Philadelphia 76ers

From the 1930s through the early 1970s, the NCAA, NBL, BAA, and NBA all agreed that no professional league would draft players who hadn't attended college or weren't at least twenty-one years old, reasoning that college ball prepares young players for the pros and that competition matures promising athletes into high-performing ones. It didn't hurt that universities made loads of money off the unpaid athletes in the process. But in the mid-1970s, a youngster from Petersburg, Virginia, by the name of Moses Malone came along and changed the rules. Moses was tearing up the high school game, leading his team to fifty straight wins and two championships, and word was that he might not play college ball. Fortunately for Moses and the game of basketball, the new American Basketball Association wasn't concerned with abiding by the old rule. It had already made an exception for players to join the league before completing college if they were having a hard time making ends meet. And Moses fit the bill. His mother was ailing, and his family needed help getting by. Going pro early made sense for him. And besides, Moses was ready.

At age nineteen, Moses was drafted by the ABA's Utah Stars, becoming the first player in the modern era to go straight to the pros out of high school. He played center and dominated from the start. He was big—six-ten and 230 pounds—and strong. He wasn't a big talker, though—he let his work on the floor speak for itself. Moses was one of the league's best rebounders and scorers. He and Julius Erving teamed up to win a championship for the Sixers in 1983. As the first high schooler to make it in pro ball, he opened doors for some of the best players in the game, like Kevin Garnett, Kobe Bryant, and LeBron James as well as dozens of other young players who would go straight to the big time.

Moses Malone

LARRY BIRD

"I didn't have the quickness; I didn't have jumping ability. I just thought the game out."

—Larry Bird, Boston Celtics

Judging from appearances, you might not think Larry Bird was a great basketball player. "Guys would ask me, 'Larry's not that good?'" Boston Celtic Cedric Maxwell recalled. "I said, 'You're gonna find out here in a minute.'" Bird was tall, thin, and scruffy looking, with blond hair and an awkward smile. He wasn't particularly muscular, and he couldn't jump to save his life. But after watching him play one game, you'd be a believer.

Every player in the league learned fast that he was one of the best sharpshooters and passers the game had ever seen. You couldn't leave him open. He'd bury you with a jumper from anywhere on the court. He even shot well with an opponent's hand in his face. He seemed to prefer it that way. He said he felt insulted if teams didn't put their best defenders on him. He'd abuse them, too. Come off a pick, catch the ball, and drain a three-pointer or do a quick turnaround jumper without cracking a smile. Bird was all business, especially in the fourth quarter. He was clutch, and his focus was uncanny. You couldn't let him get the ball for the last shot or it was game over. And let me tell you, Larry was one of the best trash-talkers in basketball. Get him started and he'd chew your ear off all game long, saying things like "Merry Christmas!" after hitting a shot. Or he might even tell you what he was going to do once he got the ball. He'd say something like "I'm going to do a step back, turn and shoot, and nail it in your face." And then he'd go and do it!

Larry was very clever, too. He could predict what *you* would do before you did it, which made him a formidable defender. He fit very well into the Celtic tradition, trusting his teammates and sharing the ball. Larry helped turn the team around after Bill Russell retired and the historic run of championships had fizzled out. Along with tough teammates like Kevin McHale, Robert Parish, Danny Ainge, and Dennis Johnson and thousands of Boston Garden's chanting fans, the mighty Celtics were tough to beat on their home court—or any court, for that matter. Larry was a certified winner, a basketball master who led his Boston Celtics to three championships. That fellow from French Lick, Indiana, was the truth.

Larry Bird

CELTICS
33

LAKERS
32

MAGIC JOHNSON

"Never fear. E.J. is here!"

—Earvin "Magic" Johnson, Los Angeles Lakers

Before Earvin Johnson Jr., there'd never been a six-foot-nine point guard in NBA history. He was nicknamed Magic by a sports columnist from the local newspaper because of his exciting, unpredictable style. Magic was a throwback to Bob Cousy and the Harlem Globetrotters, but he had a stylistic flair that was all his own. He could play any position, even center, where he would let off his baby skyhook shot, but he was most lethal as a point guard. Johnson was a true leader. He could score whenever he wanted to, but he always looked to pass the ball first, shooting only when necessary. He was one of the game's premier playmakers. Magic had all the tricks. He could make no-look and impossible threaded-needle passes, and he had great fake shots, wraparound passes, alley-oops, and assists. It was like he had eyes in the back of his head. He could always find the open man at the right time. But drop one of his passes and he'd give you the eye—you might not get the ball again for a while.

Magic and his Los Angeles Lakers, they liked to run. When they got a rebound, they were off to the races. Two or three passes, and the ball was on the other end of the court. Two points. It was something to see! Johnson had the crowd in the palm of his hand, cheering for his passes. He smiled big and showed all thirty-two pearly whites, lighting up the whole arena, having fun, slapping high fives, and hugging his teammates. It was contagious. Magic led his Lakers to five championships.

Magic was the perfect complement to Larry Bird. When they played against each other, it was competition at its best. Their rivalry began in college. The fans followed them right into the pros, where both the Lakers and the Celts were at the top of their respective divisions, having already met eight times in the finals. And all eight times, the Lakers went home winless.

Boston beat everybody. The rivalry between the Celtics and Lakers was made for television, and the network played it up: It was East vs. West. The hard-nosed Boston Celtics vs. the flashy "Showtime" Los Angeles Lakers. The old guard vs. the new one. Blue-collar vs. Hollywood. The world's best forward vs. the world's best point guard. The white country hick vs. the Black city kid. Bird vs. Magic. It was the hottest ticket in town, and fans across the country tuned in by the millions. Larry and Magic took pro basketball to the next level; they are largely responsible for the popularity of the game today. The 1980s belonged to them. The 1990s, however, belonged to someone else.

Earvin "Magic" Johnson

MICHAEL JORDAN

"People ask me, 'Do you really think you can fly?' I say, 'Yeah, for a little while.'"

—Michael Jordan, Chicago Bulls

In the history of this game, there have been many talented players who could put up big numbers, play above the rim, and win championships. But there had never been a player quite like Michael Jordan. Standing six feet, six inches tall and weighing 225 pounds, Michael was like high-flying David Thompson, smooth-sailing Elgin Baylor, and stylish Julius Erving all rolled into one. A perfect storm of fundamentally sound basketball skills, athleticism, drive, intelligence, style, and focus. When he joined the Chicago Bulls in 1985, Michael became the most exciting player that professional basketball had ever seen. He created moves in midair, doing acrobatic feats that did not seem humanly possible. While defenders were on their way down, Jordan was still ascending. Like Elgin, Michael had plenty of hang time. He could even leap high enough to hit his head on the rim or dunk from the free-throw line with a one-handed double-pump. It's why they called him Air Jordan.

Michael's game was beautiful. He would run down the court, keeping real loose, moving without the ball. And then, quick as lightning, he'd snatch the ball and blow past his man. Then he'd take off, twisting around defenders in the air, switching hands, rocking and cradling the ball like a baby, squeezing past defenders, and kissing the ball off the glass with a little English backspin on it so that it would bounce into the basket—all while taking a few chomps on his bubblegum before he hit the ground. Sometimes he'd open his mouth wide and let his tongue hang out, as though he was gawking at the move he'd just made. Give him the baseline, and he'd embarrass you. Give him the outside shot, and he'd drain it. Try to block his shot and he'd jump higher or deploy his deadly fadeaway jumper. They'd send two or three guys to guard him at once. Didn't matter—he still lit 'em up. He once dropped sixty-three points on the Celtics in a playoff game, in the Garden! *Nobody* did that. They were shocked. Bird said he was "God disguised as Michael Jordan."

Michael became a true master of the game, and what separated MJ from all the rest was that his defense was just as good as his offense. He led the league in steals, and blocked shots by players big and small. If he had a weakness, they never found it. And listen, you didn't want to make him mad. Throw any shade at MJ, and you were going to pay for it. He'd just humiliate you, and tell you about it the

Michael Jordan

whole way. Once, in the 1992 playoffs in Miami, MJ hadn't scored a basket by the start of the second quarter. A couple of younger defenders got a little too full of themselves and gave MJ a smug and scornful look. Well, Michael quickly scored, and began counting backward from forty with each made basket. Toward the end of the game, MJ had not only scored forty points on those young fellas, but he had dropped an extra sixteen more by the final buzzer, and taught them a valuable lesson: Respect your elders.

Jordan was so inspiring that he elevated the play of his teammates and led two different Chicago Bulls teams to six NBA championships in all. Often, his own teammates caught themselves *watching* him instead of playing the game, shaking their heads in disbelief at the amazing feats they'd just witnessed. Michael Jordan was an astronaut, a basketball genius who took the league from good to great; he put the NBA on his shoulders and invited the world to see what it meant to fly.

Deuce

ALLEN IVERSON

"I'm gonna let my [hair] grow out and start the season with cornrows."

—Allen Iverson, Philadelphia 76ers

As a high schooler from Hampton, Virginia, not only was Allen Iverson the best point guard in the country, but he was likely the best quarterback, too, and he brought his evasive football footwork to the NBA hardwood. After high school, Al chose to play college basketball over football and became a big star at Georgetown University, playing under Coach John Thompson. He debuted in the NBA with the Philadelphia 76ers in 1996. He was small and lean, only six feet tall and a mere 165 pounds, and a charmer with big childlike eyes. But don't let that baby face fool you. Allen Iverson was ice-cold with a basketball. He could pass like Magic, shoot like Bird, and jump like Mike, and that fellow had a devastating crossover dribble (an offensive move where the ball handler quickly changes direction while simultaneously bouncing the ball from one hand to the other). The move was so effective that they now call it the Allen Iverson Crossover.

He left many a defender off-balance, going the wrong way, or falling to the floor as though their ankles had been broken. It was something to see that little fellow weave in and out of traffic, break down the offense, and then pop up for a sweet jump shot or dish, or even a slam dunk. And boy, did Allen have heart. Outfitted with sweatbands, hidden ankle socks, oversize shorts, and arm sleeves, he went all out every time he was on the floor and never disappointed. He wore his hair braided in cornrows, and his arms, neck, and legs were all covered with tattoos. He looked like the perfect combination of hip-hop and basketball. Nobody had seen that in the pros before. Today, players all over the league are still copying his look and his moves. Just like the ink on his tattooed frame, Iverson put his stamp on the game, and after he made his mark, basketball was never the same.

Allen Iverson

LEBRON JAMES

"I never say 'myself.' I say 'my team.'"

—LeBron James, Los Angeles Lakers

At the 1984 NBA draft in New York City, the Chicago Bulls chose Michael Jordan with the third overall pick. Just six months later and some 438 miles east of Manhattan's Holland Tunnel, a seven-and-a-half pound, twenty-and-a-half-inch baby boy by the name of LeBron James was born in Akron, Ohio. Over the next seventeen years, that young fellow grew into a six-foot-nine powerhouse. Many began to refer to him as the Chosen One. Some even called him King James.

As a kid, he and his single mother battled through tough times. He found sanctuary on the basketball court with a close-knit group of friends and teammates, and together they consistently dominated the competition. From the start, James was a beast on the basketball court. He was tall. Big. And strong. He could jump out of the gym, handle the ball well, and had great court vision. He was also a tremendous scorer…but uncommon among many great scorers, LeBron passed and shared the ball just as well as he shot. And the boy could shoot. He scored easily and was a natural leader, landing no-look passes, dropping three-pointers, and dunking at will on all comers. By the time he was seventeen years old, he had appeared on the cover of *Sports Illustrated* and had grown into a basketball prodigy. In his senior year, James led his high school team to the national championship, and many predicted he would become one of basketball's greatest practitioners. He didn't disappoint.

He carried his superb skills straight from the twelfth grade right into the pros, where over the span of a twenty-plus-year career he became one of the greatest basketball players in history, dominating the league, winning multiple championships, MVP awards, and Olympic gold medals, and breaking the all-time scoring record once held by Kareem Abdul-Jabbar.

LeBron James is among the very best of the best to ever grace a basketball court, and most agree that he could have dominated in any era.

LeBron James

bibigo
LAKERS
23

STEPHEN CURRY

"When I first started…I was always the smallest kid on my team."

—Stephen Curry, Golden State Warriors

If you didn't know any better, his youthful appearance, quiet demeanor, and mere six-foot-two stature might cause you to overlook him in the team lineup. But that would be a mistake. Chef Curry, as we called him, was the real deal. One of the game's brightest and best athletes and the greatest gunner in basketball history.

Chef's workout regimen could only be described as scientific, meticulous, and intense, following a strict daily diet and workout routine that included up to five hundred made shots followed by stretching, yoga, and salt baths. His hard work and practice sculpted the youngster into tip-top shape and made his game-day performances look effortless.

Before each game, as the arena filled with fans, Chef would perform a shooting spectacle that defied the laws of physics. Beginning just a foot in front of the basket, he'd nail each shot as he moved backward to the middle of the paint, then to the free-throw line, to the three-point line, and all the way to the half-court logo, and then forward again, burying each shot on his way back to the front of the basket, where he'd throw the ball thirty feet straight into the air and watch it fall through the basket without hitting any iron. And that was just the warm-up.

During the game, he'd put on a ballhandling display that was dizzying. His quick footwork moved him past, around, and between players, back and forth, dribbling, dishing the ball, weaving through picks, squeezing through taller players to receive a pass and nail a shot with a super quick release that looked like a Hail Mary from God knows where. And he did this over and over, even past the outstretched hands of taller defenders. He routinely made baskets from ten to twenty feet *behind* the three-point line and even farther away. He'd even bury shots from the opposite side of the court or sink one from the tunnel door before heading to the locker room. Steph was operating on a whole different level. Players around the league began copying his technique, shooting from way back, and spreading the defense wide open. Kids all over the world were trying it, too. Curry made the three-point shot just as swaggy as the slam dunk.

Stephen Curry

FOURTH QUARTER

The Winning Tradition

"We win because we play together as a team."

—John Havlicek, Boston Celtics

It's pretty amazing if you think about it. Basketball grew from a slow, flat-footed game of keep-away played in a YMCA gym with a soccer ball and peach baskets to a fast-paced, high-flying spectacle, with breakaway rims, triple-post offenses, slam dunks, and thirty-foot three-point bombs, played in huge arenas all over the world. It is a beautiful thing.

When the game was first invented, it was meant to be played simply for fun, for the sport of friendly competition among amateurs. The idea was that no single player was greater than the whole. All the greatest basketball teams have embraced this concept. Some of the best include the 1966–67 Philadelphia 76ers with Wilt Chamberlain and Harold "Hal" Greer and the 1982–83 Sixers with Julius Erving and Moses Malone. The 1972–73 New York Knicks with Walt Frazier, Willis Reed, and Phil Jackson. The 1970–71 Milwaukee Bucks with Kareem Abdul-Jabbar and Oscar Robertson. The 1988–89 Detroit Pistons. The undefeated US women's national team with Lisa Leslie, Rebecca Lobo, and Sheryl Swoopes.

The Original Celtics were the first to lead the pack, setting the standard for masterful basketball and boasting a win-loss record of 193 and 11 with 1 tie for the 1922–23 season. Their top players were Henry "Dutch" Dehnert, expert ball handler Nat Holman, John Beckman, Lou Bender, and their powerful center, Joe Lapchick.

Equal in talent, but not allowed to play in the white professional leagues because of the color of their skin, was the New York Renaissance Big Five, the premier African American basketball team

Anthony Edwards of the Minnesota Timberwolves next to a mural of the 1925 New York Renaissance Big Five

during the 1920s and the strongest team in basketball in the 1930s. Some of the best players over their twenty-year heyday were Leon Monde, Wee Willie Smith, and Hall of Famers John Isaacs, Charles "Tarzan" Cooper, and Clarence "Fats" Jenkins.

The Rens were followed by the Harlem Globetrotters, whose owner, Abe Saperstein, held a monopoly on Black basketball talent for a time. Saperstein took his team on the road, touring all over the United States and overseas in Europe, Africa, Cuba, South America, and China, playing for queens, presidents, prime ministers, dictators, popes, and other world leaders. With their unconventional brand of comedy and superb basketball, they packed basketball arenas, outdoor stadiums, and makeshift basketball courts, becoming a roaring success and the ambassadors of goodwill all over the world. Over the years, their roster included Marques Haynes, Sweetwater Clifton, Lynette Woodard, Wilt Chamberlain, and even Magic Johnson. During this time, they were led by clown princes Goose Tatum, Meadowlark Lemon, and Fred "Curly" Neal. The Trotters are credited with popularizing the slam dunk and, most important, helping the struggling NBA stay afloat during its early years by playing doubleheaders to boost ticket sales. The Globetrotters are basketball royalty.

THE BOSTON CELTICS

Some say the Boston Celtics of the 1960s and 1980s are among the greatest teams of all time. They could be right. The Celts lay claim to having won eighteen championships. As one of the charter members of the Basketball Association of America, the Celtics began as a losing team in their first four seasons before hiring head coach Arnold "Red" Auerbach, a short, iron-willed basketball genius from Brooklyn, New York. Auerbach built the team into a perennial powerhouse that dominated the game like no other before it. The Celtics played unselfish basketball and were known for their mental toughness and last-second heroics. Classic contests ended with hundreds of frenzied fans storming the court, jumping up and down, celebrating to the words of the tobacco-tinged voice of announcer Johnny Most: "It's all over! It's *aaalll* over!"

Toward the end of games when they were ahead, Auerbach would often light up his famous victory cigar, irritating the opposing team while adding smoke to the misty atmosphere in the old Boston Garden, an arena famous for its patchy parquet floor with hollow dead spots, its dim lighting and lack of air-conditioning, its cramped, lockerless visitors' locker room with often cold showers, and its dedicated, boisterous, and brutal fans. Dozens of Celtics are listed in the Hall of Fame, including

2007–08 NBA champions, the Boston Celtics: Paul Pierce, Rajon Rondo, Kevin Garnett, Ray Allen, and Kendrick Perkins

PIERCE
RONDO
GARNETT
ALLEN
PERK

LAKERS
WORLD CHAMPIONS
LAKERS
WORLD CHAMPIONS
LAKERS
WORLD CHAMPIONS
LAKERS
LAKERS
LAKERS
LAKERS

Bob Cousy, Bill Russell, John Havlicek, Dave Bing, Pete Maravich, K. C. Jones, Dennis Johnson, Larry Bird, Robert Parish, and Kevin McHale. The epic matchups between the Celts and Lakers helped popularize the game and brought pro basketball into the modern era.

THE LOS ANGELES LAKERS

"The good Lord and four disciples couldn't beat the Lakers tonight," famed sportscaster Francis "Chick" Hearn often crooned. He was on to something. Despite the Lakers' modest beginnings, the team became one of the league's winningest teams. In 1960, the NBA expanded westward and the Minneapolis Lakers moved to sunny Southern California. The newly branded Los Angeles Lakers players had to drum up their own support around town. Using scripts and shouting through megaphones, they drove around Los Angeles neighborhoods inviting fans to their games: "We're going to be at the Sports Arena the next 10 days. First up, the New York Knicks. Please come and see us." It was a humble beginning for what would eventually be one of the most successful pro basketball teams in history. Elgin Baylor's and Jerry West's brilliant play helped make the team a powerhouse in the league and spurred other expansion teams in San Francisco and San Diego. Home games at the Los Angeles Sports Arena and the fabulous Forum were star-studded events with attendees the likes of movie stars Doris Day and Jack Nicholson. The Lakers were a hot ticket. Under stylish coach Pat Riley, the 1980s team ran a "Showtime" fast-break offense that wowed fans and captured the attention of the country. The Lakers organization was home to some of the game's greatest players: George Mikan, Elgin Baylor, Jerry West, Wilt Chamberlain, Kareem Abdul-Jabbar, Magic Johnson, Shaquille O'Neal, Kobe Bryant, and LeBron James. To date, the Lakers have brought home seventeen championship rings.

THE CHICAGO BULLS

After the Chicago Bulls selected Michael Jordan out of the University of North Carolina in the 1984 draft, he became the nucleus of a powerhouse team that dominated the 1990s. They won six championships over eight years, placing the Bulls among the top teams in history. Jordan, along with a host of fellow bloodthirsty coconspirators like Scottie Pippen, Steve Kerr, Bill Cartwright, John Paxson,

1999–2000, 2000–01, and 2001–02 NBA champions, the Los Angeles Lakers: Rick Fox, Derek Fisher, Shaquille O'Neal, Kobe Bryant, and Robert Horry

Dennis Rodman, Craig Hodges, Horace Grant, B. J. Armstrong, and Toni Kukoc, overran every team: the New York Knicks, the Los Angeles Lakers, the Detroit Pistons, the Miami Heat, the Indiana Pacers. The Bulls' late third-quarter surges were as dependable as clockwork and were punctuated by organ solos over the old Chicago Stadium loudspeaker system that brought the crowd to its feet in a heightened frenzy, screaming, "Da-da-da-da, da-da! Charge!" The fifteen thousand fans would bite their nails as Jordan and Pippen led the assault under the brilliant direction of head coach Phil Jackson, a former New York Knick, and offensive coach Fred "Tex" Winter, creator of a deadly offense called the triangle, the most optimal way for players to be spaced on the court while slashing, cutting, and passing. The Bulls were almost unbeatable during the 1995–96 season, setting a record of 72 wins and only 10 losses, a mark that stood for twenty years until beaten by the 2015–16 Golden State Warriors, coached by who else but former Chicago Bulls shooting guard Steve Kerr.

1995–96, 1996–97, and 1997–98 NBA champions, the Chicago Bulls: Ron Harper, Luc Longley, Michael Jordan, Dennis Rodman, and Scottie Pippen

THE DREAM TEAM

The greatest assemblage of players by far was the 1992 US men's Olympic basketball team, better known as the Dream Team. It was the first year that professional basketball players from the United States were allowed to play in Olympic competition. In Barcelona, Spain, the US men's basketball team showed the globe what the game looks like when the very best athletes in the world apply their craft on the hardwood. The squad of eleven NBA future Hall of Famers and one college standout was led by Detroit Pistons coach Chuck Daly. The players were David Robinson, Clyde Drexler, Larry Bird, Magic Johnson, Michael Jordan, Scottie Pippen, Chris Mullin, Patrick Ewing, Charles Barkley, Karl Malone, John Stockton, and college all-American Christian Laettner. Coach Daly sat back and soaked it all in. The greatest basketball players in history and a plucky collegiate star demolished competition from all corners of the earth. Twelve basketball masters. Eight games. Eight wins. Twelve gold medals. One perfect basketball team. The greatest ever.

1992 US men's Olympic basketball Dream Team

COMETS
22

OVERTIME

She Got Game: Ladies, Belles, and Ballers

"We were ladies too, we just played basketball like boys."

—Ruth Glover, Bennett College

If you can believe it, in the 1800s, the popular thinking was that women were too dainty and too weak to be "fit for exercise." Truth is, all those folks with their low opinions had no idea what women were capable of. Maybe they hadn't considered what really made playing sports so difficult for women at the time: the clothing they had to wear in order to please men. I mean, who could breathe in those tight corsets they wore around their ribs? Who could run in a long, flouncy dress? In the 1920s, when women discarded their tight corsets, traded in bulky dresses for bloomers and stockings, took up the vote, and asserted themselves in the world, the way was paved for future female athletes to step onto the court and prove they were plenty strong enough.

Women have been playing basketball since the game was invented, and from the start their games were just as competitive as the men's. Since many thought sports were "unhealthy" for young ladies, individual schools adapted Dr. Naismith's original rules differently for women. In 1899, Senda Berenson, the director of physical education at Smith College out in Northampton, Massachusetts, developed a universal set of rules for the women's game. The court was broken up into three sections, and players were confined to each one. Teams numbered at least six, up to nine. To avoid injuries, zero "roughness," like shouldering, tripping, or hacking, was allowed; and each player was permitted just three dribbles before they had to shoot or pass the ball. The women's rules made their games stately affairs, orderly and *very* slow.

Sheryl Swoopes

But rules, my young friends, are meant to be broken. In the 1930s, a new class of sportswomen leaped into the fray, and Berenson's rules were abandoned. Leading the pack was Ora Washington, a five-foot-seven muscular and lightning-quick ball hawk from Caroline County, Virginia, who played with the Germantown Hornets and the Philadelphia Tribunes. She quickly changed the perception of what women could do on a basketball court. Like her contemporary, Olympic great Mildred "Babe" Didrikson, a solid young high school cager herself, Ora was a multisport athlete and dominated women's tennis. By her twenties, she turned her attention to basketball. With her large hands and broad shoulders, Ora could sink a bucket from beyond the half-court line, pound the ball inside, or drill a running one-hander. She could pass and shoot with either hand, and she scored a career high thirty-eight points in a single game. When necessary, Washington took charge and dominated her adversaries. Once, on a jump ball, she clocked her opponent in the ribs on the way up and grabbed the ball as the young lady fell to the ground. She led her Tribunes, a professional team that often outdrew the local men's teams (even the Harlem Rens), to eleven straight championships.

During the first half of the twentieth century, women's basketball thrived in local spots like high schools, colleges, and community centers, but there weren't many other places where women could play. In the 1930s, a few women's teams began to make some traction on national college and barnstorming circuits. One of the strongest women's teams came out of Bennett College in Greensboro, North Carolina. Called the Belles, they conducted themselves like charmed socialites off the court, but on the court

Ora Washington

they were all business, winning all but one contest between 1933 and 1937. Tuskegee University in Alabama had a great team, too. Their game was like that of the Harlem Rens—full of give-and-go, in which one player passes to a teammate and immediately cuts toward the goal to receive a return pass. Oftentimes, the ball rarely hit the floor. As soon as the ball came off the rim, it was rebound, a few passes, and a quick score, all night long.

In the 1930s and '40s, most people across the country didn't have televisions, so fans were starved for entertainment. When thousands of young men began signing up for the draft and going overseas to fight the war, men's professional basketball struggled, and it created an opening for women's basketball to grow. Teams like the All American Red Heads, the Wayland Baptist Flying Queens, and the Arkansas Travelers toured the country playing for sellout crowds, which helped the game carry on. And those young ladies weren't playing by the limited women's rules. They played full court five-on-five games with men's rules, primarily against all-men teams.

The women's teams were sponsored by organizations or colleges, and they played in the Amateur Athletic Union (AAU), the only league for women at the time. In the 1950s, the AAU was dominated by the Flying Queens, which traveled to games by plane, a very rare thing in those days. The best player in the league, by far, was a six-foot-one country gal from Tennessee by the name of Nera White. She played for the Nashville Business College, and some folks say she was the greatest female basketball player ever. Nera was as strong as a large man and could shoot from all corners of the court, even from a step over the half-court line. Shame it only counted for two points (there was no

Nera White

All American Red Heads

LESLIE
9
AZZI
8
BOLTON
USA

three-point line then). She could jump higher and run faster than anybody in the AAU and could even slam-dunk. She often drove toward the basket, then jumped from the free-throw line and glided to the rim for an easy layup. When opposing teams tried to press, Nera's teammates just gave her the ball, and she pushed right through. Nera was a powerhouse. She was named all-American fifteen times, more than any female player before or since.

By the late 1950s, women's basketball was on the decline. After the war ended and the troops came home, male attitudes toward female roles changed. Husbands wanted their wives to be at home, not out working. Watching women play sports was no longer a popular pastime, and young girls were discouraged from following that career path. Aside from a few pockets around the country, substantially fewer girls were playing the game.

It wasn't until the early 1970s that the ball started rolling again. Congress passed Title IX, which required schools to fund men's and women's sports equally, and thousands of young women started graduating from college with sharp basketball skills. The most talented were offered opportunities to play on the brand-new women's Olympic basketball team in 1976 and in the Women's Professional Basketball League that started in 1978. The women's game was finally growing.

Still, women's pro ball struggled. Although the game had its share of stars, ticket sales sagged, and the Women's Professional Basketball League folded in 1981. Other attempts to start a women's pro league in the United States failed as well, forcing players to look for international opportunities after college. The foreign leagues paid pretty well, but if players didn't speak the local language, they felt isolated. Those who couldn't play overseas quit altogether.

The door to women's pro ball swung back open in the 1990s when the strongest college players were invited to compete in the 1996 Olympic Games in Atlanta, Georgia—athletes the likes of Texas Tech's Sheryl Swoopes, who dropped forty-seven points in the 1993 NCAA title game; Rebecca Lobo, who led the UConn Huskies to an undefeated season and championship in 1995; and six-foot-five Lisa Leslie, who dominated the boards and helped her USC Trojans take home a conference championship trophy.

That 1996 Olympic crew—the women's version of the Dream Team—kicked the tar out of every opponent they faced. Up to and including the Olympics, they played sixty games and won all of them, taking home the gold. On the heels of the Olympic games, three new professional basketball leagues for women debuted: the women's American Basketball League in 1996, the Women's National Basketball Association (WNBA) in 1997, and the National Women's Basketball League in 1998.

1996 US women's Olympic basketball team

The American Basketball League initially had the best talent, but unfortunately, the league didn't have the resources to stay in business. It only lasted two and a half years. When it folded, most of its players went over to the WNBA. The National Women's Basketball League closed in 2007.

The WNBA is now home to the top women's basketball talent in the world. They play a fast, full-contact, horizontal game with a lot of ball movement, sharp passing, cutting, and strategy. Not so different from the old Original Celtics. You won't see as many slam dunks in the women's game as the men's, but I'll tell you, that is changing. After Nera White, Cheryl Miller was the next woman to slam-dunk, in the 1980s. (Miller is, hands down, one of the greatest women basketball players in history; she once scored 105 points in a high school game.) Lisa Leslie dunked in a WNBA game in 2002, followed by Michelle Snow, Candace Parker, Sylvia Fowles, and Brittney Griner, who has dunked more often than any other female athlete. The way young women are growing and training these days, there's no doubt that soon there will be so many more playing well above the rim.

Today, professional women's basketball is growing. Although the WNBA is a relatively young league, with exciting players like Angel

Reese, Caitlin Clark, and A'ja Wilson, the women's game has exploded in popularity, attendance is solid, player salaries are increasing, and the talent level remains at its highest ever. Girls around the globe with athletic prowess, a knack for hard work, and hoop dreams can very well find a home in women's pro ball. And rightly so. They got game.

The old and new schools of women's basketball: Agnes Morley, Ruth Glover, Mildred "Babe" Didrikson, Hazel Walker, Missouri Arledge, Cheryl Miller, Cynthia Cooper, Lisa Leslie, Diana Taurasi, A'ja Wilson, and Brittney Griner

POSTGAME

The Great Game

"In no other game is co-operation so necessary." —Dr. James Naismith

Basketball began as a segregated sport, separated by neighborhoods, towns, leagues, laws, and customs. Teams were white, Jewish, and African American. Games were played indoors and outdoors. Leagues were college, semipro, and professional. They played in the East, West, North, and South. Each was unique. Each developed on its own.

Dr. Naismith created the foundation, and Dr. Henderson and Senda Berenson helped spread the word. The stage was set for the greatest athletes in the world to play out our national story. Over the course of fifty years, the game ultimately found common ground, blending its separated parts to become the great American game of basketball. A potent combination of playing styles and cultures old and new, fast and slow, horizontal and vertical, deliberate and improvised, classically proficient and jazzily virtuous, athletic and strategic, swagger filled and fundamental. Basketball. The team game.

After all these years, basketball remains the same game—put the ball into the basket. Whoever scores the most points by the time the clock runs out wins. The greatest players have taken the sport to new heights and inspired us to go even further. George Mikan, Joe Lapchick, Bob Cousy, Ora Washington, Marques Haynes, Goose Tatum, Oscar Robertson, Bill Russell, Nera White, Dan Issel, George Gervin, Earl Monroe, Moses Malone, Bob Pettit, John Stockton, Elgin Baylor, Kevin McHale, Dave Bing, Julius Erving, Larry Bird, Isiah Thomas, Lisa Leslie, Sue Bird, Hakeem Olajuwon, Rick Barry, Steve Nash, Magic Johnson, Cheryl Miller, James Worthy, Bill Sharman, Kareem Abdul-Jabbar, Shaquille O'Neal, Jerry West, Pete Maravich, Diana Taurasi, Michael Jordan, Scottie Pippen, Cynthia Cooper, Sheryl Swoopes, Allen Iverson, Kobe Bryant, LeBron James, Steph Curry. The list goes on.

The future

Although for many years African Americans were forced to play on the sidelines, we were not discouraged. We knew that we could play as well as anybody and that someday things would change. On the hardwood, it doesn't matter who your parents are. It doesn't matter how tall or short you are, or what you look like. All that matters is whether you can play.

Basketball is basketball. It is said that basketball doesn't build character, it reveals it. It reminds us that basketball is a team sport that functions at its peak when every player can contribute. It's not so different from the game of life. Every player is essential to the whole. The best fives. The best players. The best teams. All love the game. We all need each other. And this game is more fun when we can all play together. Amen and Game On.

AUTHOR'S NOTE

I remember holding a basketball for the very first time. I was about four years old, and my uncle handed me a ball from a game he'd just played on a neighborhood court. The orange-brown leather was moist and worn. I pushed it down toward the ground, and it bounced back up into my hands. It was love at first dribble.

I began playing regularly at ten years old and joined the high school team at fifteen. By then, my bedroom walls were decorated with posters, memorabilia, and drawings and paintings I'd made of my basketball hero, Michael Jordan. In my ninth-grade year, Michael was in my hometown for a celebrity golf tournament, and my mother took my little brother and me to the event with the hope that we might meet him. While we stood near one of the holes on the course, I was excited to see another of my basketball heroes sitting in a golf cart behind us. It was Julius "Dr. J" Erving. I couldn't believe it. I nervously approached him and asked him to sign some of my drawings that I'd brought along. He very kindly obliged, telling me that my drawings had a "nice touch," and I shook his giant hand, which was so large that his fingertips reached almost halfway to my elbow.

Just then, we spotted Michael on a golf cart, and we flagged him and his driver down. While my mother engaged Michael's driver in a conversation, I had a moment to speak to Michael one-on-one. I remember being quite tongue-tied and shy, and impressed with his physicality and very dark, flawless skin. I looked down at his large white golf shoes and finally mustered a few words. "Michael, what shoe size do you wear?" He smiled wide. "Thirteen," he said. He signed my drawings and was quickly whisked away by the driver. I could have died a happy teenager.

I continued to play basketball in college while I studied art at Pratt Institute in Brooklyn, New York. When I look back at my development as an artist and athlete, I can fully appreciate how both disciplines enriched my understanding of physical movement, and particularly how my participation in sports informed my ability to communicate energy in motion through the painted medium. For this book, I endeavored to create a dynamic blend of literature, visual art, and athletics to tell the great story of basketball.

One of the most difficult challenges of telling this story was condensing the sport's long history into a mere 112 pages of text and artwork and to create an aesthetic that encompassed both the old and new schools of basketball. To do this, I pored over vintage sports catalogs and publications; visited museum collections; studied numerous written and oral histories, including articles, biographies, and autobiographies; and combed through documentaries and interviews with players and coaches while also drawing upon my own personal experiences in basketball, both on and off the court. I focused on the game's origins and followed its professional evolution to the present day, but had I been able to create a book double in length, I would have chosen to expand significantly the stories of street and college basketball as well as the women's game, all of which have fascinating histories of their own. The evolution of women's basketball, in particular, continues to be an ever-expanding and rapidly developing component of the sport's story.

I felt the most intriguing method of sharing this story would be through the sage voice of a fictional narrator with a familial tone, not unlike that of the elders from my formative years, who speaks from the firsthand experiences of a former basketball player who's witnessed the game evolve from its humble beginnings on a college campus into a flashy athletic spectacle on the world stage.

Often, books about sports history rely on existing photographs to accompany the written word. As a painter, I have the benefit of being able to create unique visuals to complement the text, primarily by utilizing vintage photographs for reference and historical accuracy. For some of the paintings—especially those set in the late 1800s through the mid-1950s, before the game became widely covered and photographed by the news media—photographic references were limited or even nonexistent. For example, photographs of the earliest basketball games at the International YMCA Training School proved elusive, so creating a painting of on-court action was quite challenging. I found a single group photo depicting Dr. Naismith's first YMCA men's team and a single photo of the school's storied gym. To compose the players in the painting, I relied on quirky, old-fashioned photographs and paintings of a variety of athletes from the turn of the century. This process was like conducting a treasure hunt for sports artifacts and photos, and often yielded rewarding results.

For me, this book is a love letter to its namesake. It's an ambitious work that celebrates not only the story and impact of the game but also its athletic and cultural revolutionaries, whose gigantic feats and figures are often—and very intentionally—too large to fit on the page. I hold the game of basketball in very high esteem, mostly because it is an essential part of my personal and professional evolution as an artist and human being. Perhaps that is why I spent almost a decade honing the text and creating over sixty original oil paintings that pay tribute to the sport. Both on and off the court, basketball taught me about teamwork, camaraderie, energy, and physical and artistic expression. That's the essence of what makes basketball arguably the greatest game ever created. I hope that the lessons of the game will continue to inspire readers and athletes for generations to come.

TIMELINE

1891 First basketball game takes place at International YMCA Training School in Springfield, Massachusetts.

1893 First college games are played. Both Vanderbilt University in Nashville and Geneva College in Pennsylvania play teams from local YMCAs.

1896 First basketball game where players are paid to play takes place in Trenton, New Jersey.

1898 National Basketball League, the first pro league, begins play with teams from Philadelphia and New Jersey. League disbands in 1904.

1902 Eighteen-year-old **Bucky Lew** of Lowell, Massachusetts, becomes first Black man to play professional basketball.

1904 **Edwin B. Henderson** introduces basketball to Black students in Washington, DC.

Nation's first all-Black fitness club, the Alpha Physical Culture Club, is founded in Harlem.

1907 Smart Set Athletic Club in Brooklyn forms first organized Black basketball team. St. Christopher Club in Manhattan soon follows.

First game of all-Black Olympian Athletic League takes place at Knickerbocker Basketball Court in Brooklyn.

1910 First African American professional basketball team, the New York All Stars, forms in Harlem. Team disbands after three seasons.

1920s All-white Original Celtics from New York dominate pro basketball, recording 193 wins, 11 losses, and 1 tie in 1922–23 season alone.

1923 All-Black New York Renaissance Big Five is founded in Harlem. Rens regularly play Original Celtics throughout the 1920s.

1926 Harlem Globetrotters are founded in Chicago. First game is played January 7, 1927, in Hinckley, Illinois.

1930s Jump shot emerges in college game with shooters like **Glenn Roberts**, **Hank Luisetti**, and **Kenny Sailors**.

1937–38 New National Basketball League plays first season with thirteen teams in the Midwest.

1939 Rens defeat Globetrotters in semifinal of first World's Championship of Professional Basketball tournament and go on to beat Oshkosh All Stars for title.

1940 Globetrotters defeat Rens in semifinals of professional tournament and beat Chicago Bruins for world title.

1942–43 National Basketball League integrates for one season.

1946 **George Mikan** signs with Chicago Gears of National Basketball League.

Basketball Association of America is founded with eleven big-city teams, including New York Knicks, Boston Celtics, Chicago Stags, and Philadelphia Warriors.

1947 Detroit Gems move to Minneapolis, become Lakers, and acquire **Mikan**.

1948 Globetrotters defeat Lakers in exhibition game before Chicago crowd of 17,823.

Lakers win National Basketball League title, defeating Rochester Royals.

Lakers, Rochester Royals, Fort Wayne Pistons, and Indianapolis Kautskys leave National Basketball League for Basketball Association of America.

Rens join National Basketball League and move to Dayton, Ohio.

1949 Globetrotters defeat Lakers again in Chicago exhibition.

Lakers win Basketball Association of America title, defeating Washington Capitols.

National Basketball League and Basketball Association of America merge to create the NBA, with seventeen teams. No Black players are allowed. Dayton Rens are excluded from merger, and team folds.

1950 Lakers defeat Globetrotters in two exhibition games.

Bob Cousy is drafted fourth overall by Tri-Cities Blackhawks, ends up in Boston.

NBA integrates with drafting of **Chuck Cooper** by Boston Celtics and **Earl Lloyd** by Washington Capitols. Globetrotters' **Nat Clifton** joins New York Knicks; **Hank DeZonie** joins Tri-Cities Blackhawks.

1951 East beats West in first NBA All-Star Game, held at Boston Garden.

Free-throw lane is widened from six feet to twelve feet.

1954 Shot clock is introduced in pro game.

1956 **Bill Russell** is drafted second overall

by St. Louis Hawks and traded to Boston Celtics.

1958 **Elgin Baylor** is drafted first overall by Minneapolis Lakers.

1959 **Wilt Chamberlain** is drafted third overall by Philadelphia Warriors.

1960s Boston Celtics dominate NBA, winning nine championships.

1960 Minneapolis Lakers move to Los Angeles.

Oscar Robertson is drafted first overall by Cincinnati Royals; Lakers take **Jerry West** second.

1961 NBA adds Chicago Packers as expansion team.

1962 **Chamberlain** scores one hundred points against New York Knicks on March 2.

1962–63 **Robertson** averages triple-double for season; **Chamberlain** averages fifty points per game.

1963 Philadelphia Warriors move to San Francisco.

Chicago Zephyrs (formerly Packers) move to Baltimore, become Bullets. Syracuse Nationals move to Philadelphia, become 76ers.

1964–65 Free-throw lane is widened again, from twelve to sixteen feet.

1966 NBA adds Chicago Bulls as expansion team.

1967 ABA begins play with eleven teams.

NBA adds San Diego Rockets and Seattle SuperSonics as expansion teams.

1968 NBA adds Milwaukee Bucks and Phoenix Suns as expansion teams.

1969 **Kareem Abdul-Jabbar** is drafted first overall by Milwaukee Bucks.

1970 NBA adds Buffalo Braves, Cleveland Cavaliers, and Portland Trail Blazers as expansion teams.

1971 **Julius Erving** signs with ABA's Virginia Squires.

1974 NBA adds New Orleans Jazz as expansion team.

Moses Malone is drafted by Utah Stars in third round of ABA draft.

1976 **Erving** wins first slam dunk contest at ABA All-Star Game.

ABA is absorbed by NBA.

1978 **Larry Bird** is drafted sixth overall by Boston Celtics.

1979 **Magic Johnson** and Michigan State defeat **Larry Bird** and Indiana State in NCAA championship game.

Magic Johnson is drafted first overall by Los Angeles Lakers.

NBA adopts three-point line.

1980 NBA adds Dallas Mavericks as expansion team.

1984 **Larry Nance** wins NBA's first slam dunk contest.

Michael Jordan is drafted third overall by Chicago Bulls.

1988 NBA adds Miami Heat and Charlotte Hornets as expansion teams.

1989 NBA adds Orlando Magic and Minnesota Timberwolves as expansion teams.

1992 Men's Dream Team wins Olympic gold with **David Robinson**, **Clyde Drexler**, **Larry Bird**, **Magic Johnson**, **Michael Jordan**, **Scottie Pippen**, **Chris Mullin**, **Patrick Ewing**, **Charles Barkley**, **Karl Malone**, **John Stockton**, and **Christian Laettner**.

1995 NBA adds Toronto Raptors and Vancouver Grizzlies as expansion teams.

1996 Chicago Bulls break record for best single season with 72 wins, 10 losses.

Women's Dream Team wins Olympic gold with **Teresa Edwards**, **Ruthie Bolton-Holifield**, **Sheryl Swoopes**, **Lisa Leslie**, **Katrina McClain**, **Dawn Staley**, **Jennifer Azzi**, **Carla McGhee**, **Katy Steding**, **Rebecca Lobo**, **Venus Lacy**, and **Nikki McCray**.

Allen Iverson is drafted first overall by Philadelphia 76ers.

1997 WNBA begins play with eight teams.

2002 NBA adds New Orleans Hornets (later Pelicans) as expansion team.

2003 **LeBron James** is drafted first overall by Cleveland Cavaliers.

2008 Seattle SuperSonics relocate to Oklahoma City, become Thunder.

2009 **Stephen Curry** is drafted seventh overall by Golden State Warriors.

2016 Golden State Warriors break record for best single season with 73 wins, 9 losses.

2020 NBA suspends operations due to COVID-19 pandemic; play resumes in summer with regular season, playoffs, and finals in biosecure "bubble."

2023 **LeBron James** passes **Abdul-Jabbar** as NBA's all-time regular season scoring leader, ends twentieth season with 38,652 career points.

2024 Boston Celtics win NBA record eighteenth championship.

GLOSSARY OF BASKETBALL TERMS

all-American: A player who is voted one of the best high school or college athletes in the country

all-star: A player who is designated one of the best players on a team or in a league

alley-oop: An offensive play in which a player throws the ball to a teammate near the basket; the teammate catches the ball in midair and immediately shoots or dunks it before returning to the ground

assist: A pass to a teammate that leads directly to a scored basket

backboard: A large upright panel (typically rectangular and made of wood, glass, or metal) to which a basketball hoop is attached

baseline: The out-of-bounds line underneath each basket (also called the end line)

bench: A row of seats on the sideline where substitute players must sit during regulation play

block: A shot attempt that is deflected by an opposing player

board: Short for *backboard*; a colloquial term for a rebound

bucket: A made shot; the basket

cager: A basketball player; this term began when professional basketball was played on a court surrounded by a metal cage or rope netting

charge: A foul in which a defender standing still is run over by an offensive player who has the ball

crossover: An offensive move in which the ball handler quickly changes direction while simultaneously bouncing the ball from one hand to the other

cut: The movement of a player who makes a concerted effort to cross the court with the intention of getting open to receive a pass or drawing a defensive player away from a teammate

defense: A system of guarding players who have possession of the ball; the team without possession of the ball

dish: To pass the ball; a colloquial term for an assist

double dribble: To bounce the ball after having picked up one's dribble; to continuously dribble the ball simultaneously with both hands; an illegal move

drain: To score a shot from a distance

elbow: To drive one's elbow into another player's body; the court area where the free-throw line meets the side of the key

fadeaway: A shot where a player jumps and shoots the ball while leaning backward, away from the basket (also called a fallaway)

fast break: An offensive play in which a team attempts to move the ball to the opposite end of the court as quickly as possible after a missed shot by the opposing team, with the intention of scoring before the defense can set up

finger roll: A shot in which a player releases the ball by letting it roll off their fingertips, allowing it to arc into the basket without touching the backboard

floater: A one-handed shot, taken by a driving player who is too close for a jump shot and too far away for a layup, that arcs high over the reach of defending players (also called a teardrop)

free throw: An uncontested shot taken from the foul line after a violation (also called a foul shot)

free-throw line: The line fifteen feet from the basket from which free throws are taken (also called the foul line)

give-and-go: An offensive play in which a player passes the ball to a teammate and then immediately cuts toward the basket to receive a return pass

glass: See **backboard**

half-court: The line that divides the court into two equal parts; the playing area of each half

hang time: The time a player spends in the air between liftoff and landing

inbound: To throw the ball from the out-of-bounds area into play

jump ball: A ball put into play by the referee, who tosses it up between two opposing players

jump shot: A shot taken while springing up (also called a jumper)

key: The rectangle, sometimes painted, between the basket and the free-throw line (also called the paint or lane)

lane: See **key**

layup: A driving shot tossed up, usually with one hand, from underneath or beside the basket

man-to-man: A system in which each player on a team is assigned to defend an offensive player on the opposing team

nail: To score a basket from a distance

offense: The system of moving the ball around the court with the intention of scoring; the team with possession of the ball

out-of-bounds: The area outside of the regulation play area

paint: See **key**

palming: Holding the ball by its underside between dribbles

pass: To throw the ball to a teammate in a controlled manner

pick: A player without the ball who intentionally stands and blocks the defender of a teammate (also called a screen)

pivot: To keep one foot in place while moving the other; the stationary foot is called the pivot foot

post: The area underneath the basket at the bottom of the key; used to describe a player, usually the center, who plays in that area

rebound: To grab and gain possession of the ball after a missed shot

reverse: A layup tossed backward over one's shoulder or head

shot clock: A timer that counts down the seconds the offense has to shoot the ball before losing possession

slam-dunk: To forcefully throw the ball through the hoop and grab the rim (also called a jam)

swish: When the ball goes through the net cleanly, without touching the rim or backboard

teardrop: See **floater**

threaded-needle: A precise pass thrown through moving defenders

three-point line: The arc beyond the key separating the two-point shooting area from the three-point shooting area (the distance from the basket depends on the league)

three-second rule: The maximum amount of time any offensive player may spend inside the key before having to exit and re-enter

travel: To run or walk with the basketball without dribbling; an illegal move

triangle offense: A complex system of optimal spacing and player movement that creates scoring opportunities (also called a triple-post offense)

triple-double: Double-digit statistics in three separate categories in a single game (in points, assists, rebounds, steals, or blocks)

zone defense: A system in which defenders cover only an allotted section of the court when opponents are in their area

NOTES

1 "I've got it!": Naismith, *Basketball: Its Origin and Development*, 46.

2 "The sole object of the gentle pastime": Peterson, *Cages to Jump Shots*, 22.

2 "No shouldering, holding, pushing": Naismith, *Basketball: Its Origin and Development*, 54.

13 "Like the rest of the fellows": Peterson, *Cages to Jump Shots*, 55.

17 "The ball can travel faster": Thomas, *They Cleared the Lane*, 9.

20 "It was the Rens, not the Knicks": Mallozzi, "John Isaacs," *New York Times*.

24 "In the very beginning, I didn't know": Abdul-Jabbar, *Kareem*, 159.

29 "All those things you read about ": Finn, "Bucky Lew First Negro," *Springfield Union*.

30 "We don't accept blacks": Peterson, *Cages to Jump Shots*, 130.

39 "My game really takes off ": Erving, *Dr. J*, 79.

40 "We were ahead of the NBA": Pluto, *Loose Balls*, 29.

40 "It was a crazy league": Rick Barry, "Hall of Famer Rick Barry talks on how Dennis Murphy's ABA improved salaries for the NBA," Afterburner Enterprises, posted July 20, 2012, YouTube, https://youtu.be/9TJttheWuMc.

47 "Everybody in the NBA is good": GQ Editors, "Because I'm Kyrie," *GQ*.

49 "I had never seen a blocked shot": Russell, *Red and Me*, 25.

51 "[I'm] the villain of the NBA": Chamberlain and Shaw, *Wilt*, 170.

52 "I loved hearing the clock go down": West and Coleman, *West by West*, 30.

54 "My athletic ability": Robertson, *The Big O*, 87.

56 "'How many points you gonna score tonight?'": Gross, "Elgin Baylor," *Sport*.

58 "When the skyhook is working": Abdul-Jabbar, *Kareem*, 170.

60 "Call me the Doctor": Erving, *Dr. J*, 187.

63 "I want the ball": Moses Malone, "Moses E. Malone's Basketball Hall of Fame Enshrinement Speech," OfficialHoophall, posted June 4, 2012, YouTube, https://youtu.be/HPyVJjs1zxc.

64 "I didn't have the quickness": *Magic & Bird: A Courtship of Rivals* at 14:54.

64 "Guys would ask me": *30 for 30: Celtics/Lakers*, pt. 1, at 53:30.

67 "Never fear. E.J. is here!": Bird and Johnson, *When the Game Was Ours*, 61.

68 "People ask me": *Michael Jordan: Come Fly with Me* at 34:45.

68 "God disguised as Michael Jordan": Ryan, "The Show Is Jordan's," *Boston Globe*.

71 "I'm gonna let my [hair] grow out": Platt, *Only the Strong Survive*, 132.

72 "I never say 'myself'": LeBron James, "LeBron First Interview, What He Says Has Come True!," PHP, posted December 13, 2018, YouTube, https://youtu.be/zy7F5d4ANhY.

74 "When I first started": Stephen Curry, "Stephen Curry: I was always the smallest kid on my team," Graham Bensinger, posted February 25, 2016, YouTube, https://youtu.be/95m_zs4b0S0.

77 "We win because we play together": Murray, *129 Greatest Basketball Quotes*, 18.

81 "We're going to be at the Sports Arena": Dwyre, "Elgin Baylor," *Los Angeles Times*.

85 "We were ladies too": Liberti, "'We Were Ladies,'" *Journal of Sport History*, 575.

93 "In no other game": Naismith, *Basketball*, 185.

SOURCES

BOOKS

Abdul-Jabbar, Kareem. *Kareem*. With Mignon McCarthy. New York: Random House, 1990.

Ashe, Arthur R., Jr. *A Hard Road to Glory: A History of the African-American Athlete Since 1946*. New York: Warner Books, 1988.

Baker, Christine A. *Why She Plays: The World of Women's Basketball*. Lincoln: University of Nebraska Press, 2008.

Barkley, Charles. *I May Be Wrong but I Doubt It*. Edited by Michael Wilbon. New York: Random House, 2002.

Bird, Larry, and Earvin "Magic" Johnson. *When the Game Was Ours*. With Jackie MacMullan. New York: Mariner Books, 2010.

Butler, Robbie. *The Harlem Globetrotters: Clown Princes of Basketball*. Mankato, MN: Capstone Press, 2002.

Chamberlain, Wilt, and David Shaw. *Wilt: Just Like Any Other 7-Foot Black Millionaire Who Lives Next Door*. New York: MacMillan, 1973.

Cousy, Bob. *Basketball Is My Life*. With Al Hirshberg. Englewood Cliffs, NJ: Prentice-Hall, 1958.

Erving, Julius. *Dr. J: The Autobiography*. With Karl Taro Greenfield. New York: HarperCollins, 2013.

FreeDarko. *The Undisputed Guide to Pro Basketball History*. New York: Bloomsbury, 2010.

Grundy, Pamela, and Susan Shackelford. *Shattering the Glass: The Remarkable History of Women's Basketball*. Chapel Hill: University of North Carolina Press, 2005.

Jackson, Phil. *Sacred Hoops: Spiritual Lessons of a Hardwood Warrior*. With Hugh Delehanty. New York: Hyperion, 1995.

Johnson, Claude. *Black Fives: The Alpha Physical Culture Club's Pioneering African American Basketball Team, 1904–1923*. Greenwich, CT: Black Fives Publishing, 2012.

Jordan, Michael. *Driven from Within*. Edited by Mark Vancil. New York: Atria Books, 2005.

Jordan, Michael. *For the Love of the Game: My Story*. Edited by Mark Vancil. New York: Crown, 1998.

Lazenby, Roland. *Michael Jordan: The Life*. New York: Little, Brown, 2014.

Leslie, Lisa. *Don't Let the Lipstick Fool You*. With Larry Burnett. New York: Kensington Books, 2008.

Liberti, Rita. "'We Were Ladies, We Just Played Basketball Like Boys': African American Womanhood and Competitive Basketball at Bennett College, 1928–1942." In *Journal of Sport History* 26, no. 3 (1999): 567–584. Champaign: University of Illinois Press, 1999.

Molina, John. *Barnstorming America: Stories from the Pioneers of Women's Basketball*. With Charles A. Francis. Morley, MO: Acclaim Press, 2016.

Murray, Adam E. *129 Greatest Basketball Quotes from the Game's Most Famous People*. Self-published, CreateSpace, 2012.

Naismith, James. *Basketball: Its Origin and Development*. New York: Association Press, 1941.

Peterson, Robert W. *Cages to Jump Shots: Pro Basketball's Early Years*. New York: Oxford University Press, 1990.

Platt, Larry. *Only the Strong Survive: The Odyssey of Allen Iverson*. New York: HarperCollins, 2003.

Pluto, Terry. *Loose Balls: The Short, Wild Life of the American Basketball Association—As Told by the Players, Coaches, and Movers and Shakers Who Made It Happen*. New York: Simon & Schuster, 1990.

Reynolds, Bill. *Cousy: His Life, Career, and the Birth of Big-Time Basketball*. New York: Simon & Schuster, 2005.

Robertson, Oscar. *The Big O: My Life, My Times, My Game*. Lincoln, NE: Bison Books, 2010.

Rosen, Charley. *The First Tip-Off: The Incredible Story of the Birth of the NBA*. New York: McGraw-Hill, 2009.

Russell, Bill. *Red and Me: My Coach, My Lifelong Friend*. With Alan Steinberg. New York: HarperCollins, 2009.

Russell, Bill. *Russell Rules*. With David Falkner. New York: Dutton, 2001.

Simmons, Bill. *The Book of Basketball: The NBA According to the Sports Guy*. New York: Ballantine Books, 2009.

Sports Illustrated. *The Basketball Book*. New York: Sports Illustrated, 2007.

Surdam, David George. *The Rise of the National Basketball Association*. Urbana: University of Illinois Press, 2012.

Thomas, Ron. *They Cleared the Lane: The NBA's Black Pioneers*. Lincoln: University of Nebraska Press, 2002.

West, Jerry, and Jonathan Coleman. *West by West: My Charmed, Tormented Life*. New York: Little, Brown, 2011.

Wideman, John Edgar. "Michael Jordan Leaps the Great Divide." In *Signifiyin(g), Sanctifyin' & Slam Dunking: A Reader in African American Expressive Culture*, edited by Gena Dagel Caponi, 388–406. Amherst: University of Massachusetts Press, 1999.

FILM AND TELEVISION

30 for 30: Bad Boys. ESPN Films, 2014.

30 for 30: Celtics/Lakers: Best of Enemies. ESPN Films, 2017.

30 for 30: Free Spirits. ESPN Films, 2013.

Bill Russell: My Life, My Way. HBO Sports, 2000.

Doin' It in the Park: Pick-Up Basketball, New York City. Goldcrest Films, 2012.

The Doctor. NBA TV, 2013.

Fathers of the Sport. Gravitas Ventures, 2008.

Harlem Globetrotters: The Team That Changed the World. TeamWorks Media, 2005.

Iverson. 214 Films Entertainment Group, 2014.

Magic & Bird: A Courtship of Rivals. HBO, 2010.

Michael Jordan: Come Fly with Me. Fox Home Entertainment, 1989.

On the Shoulders of Giants. Iconomy, 2011.

The Renegade League. Afterburner Enterprises, 2012.

ARTICLES

Dwyre, Bill. "Elgin Baylor and Jerry West Are Back Together Again." *Los Angeles Times*, February 5, 2009.

Finn, Gerry. "Bucky Lew First Negro in Pro Basketball." *Springfield Union*, April 2, 1958.

FitzGerald, Tom. "With 1 Hand, Stanford's Hank Luisetti Pushed Basketball Forward." *San Francisco Chronicle*, September 4, 2015.

GQ Editors. "Because I'm Kyrie: A GQA with the NBA's Rookie of the Year." *GQ*, May 18, 2012.

Gross, Milton. "Elgin Baylor and Basketball's Big Explosion." *Sport*, April 1961.

Mallozzi, Vincent M. "John Isaacs, Star for Rens Basketball Team, Dies at 93." *New York Times*, February 3, 2009.

Martin, Douglas. "Bud Palmer, Jump Shot Pioneer, Dies at 91." *New York Times*, March 22, 2013.

McDonald, William. "Kenny Sailors, a Pioneer of the Jump Shot, Dies at 95." *New York Times*, January 30, 2016.

Pennington, Bill. "In Search of the First Jump Shot." *New York Times*, April 2, 2011.

Roberts, Sam. "Nera White, Hall of Fame Basketball Star of 1950s and '60s, Is Dead at 80." *New York Times*, April 16, 2016.

Ryan, Bob. "The Show Is Jordan's—But Celtics Steal It." *Boston Globe*, April 21, 1986.

INDEX

Page numbers in italics refer to paintings.